Zen Sleep

Enlightenment for a Good Night's Rest

Eric Chiles

ISBN 0-9723950-1-6
LCCN: 2002094046

Editorial Services by Present Perfect Books , Lake Junaluska, NC
Design by Design Den, Spokane, WA
Illustrations by Shari Jones, Denver, CO

This book is dedicated to my sister,
who shares my longing
for life's more substantial truths.

Contents

*To carry yourself forward and experience myriad things
        is delusion;
That myriad things come forth and experience themselves
        is awakening.*

Preface

At first, his words were hard to make out in the bustle of customers and the clatter of dishes in that downtown coffee shop. My Zen Buddhist friend and I were discussing insomnia: I was describing my nightly struggle to get to sleep, and how insomnia had been making my life miserable for several years.

He listened patiently at first, expressing his usual sympathy, then gradually became annoyed. Finally, he stared at me and said, "Why don't you just stop trying so hard, and let sleep do whatever it does?"

My initial reaction was to smile, roll my eyes upwards in a "here-we-go-again" expression, and automatically dismiss his suggestion. I often did that when he dropped bits of his Zen philosophy into our conversations. I never really gave them serious consideration, because frankly my friend's happy-go-lucky attitude had always seemed naïve to me. But this time, for some reason, he struck a chord.

Maybe it was because I was becoming utterly desperate to find some relief from the misery of insomnia that impacted so much of my life. I had tried prescription sleeping pills, followed all the advice my doctors gave me, and read every book on sleep I could get my hands on. Nothing had worked.

Was it sheer exhaustion that made me do a mental double-take that day, to sit up and take notice of something I otherwise would have ignored? "Stop trying what?" I asked my friend, my cynicism in temporary remission.

"To control sleep," he replied.

At first, I denied that I was trying to control anything: I suffered from insomnia, which is a medical condition requiring treatment. He just smiled and changed the subject, frustrating me with his unwillingness to elaborate. So I challenged him again to explain how I was trying to control sleep. That was easy: he simply repeated back to me all the things my doctors had recommended and I had tried. By the time we got our check, it was obvious that my friend was correct. Everything I had done thus far was, in hindsight, an attempt to control sleep. I was trying to make it happen in a certain way and at a certain time.

Here in front of me was an idea that had never occurred to me before: why not just stop trying to control sleep, and let it do whatever it does? It sounded too simple to take seriously — and at the same time, it was too profound to ignore. All of my energy had been focused for so long on obtaining sleep that the option to "Stop trying" didn't even register. It simply did not fit my view of the situation.

Was this really the direction I wanted to take? I thought back over the many times my friend had tried to explain Zen Buddhism to me. My understanding was rather limited, but I knew that the approach somehow favored direct experience over intellectual pursuit. Dissatisfaction and suffering are said to originate from the mind's insistence that the reality of the present moment be something other than what it is. Enlightenment, a concept I'd never given any credence, was obtained by directly apprehending this cause of suffering and thereby becoming free from the mind's tyranny. The mind is what torments us in the first place — or so said the Buddha.

As I sat there staring into my empty coffee cup, considering the possibility that such a hands-off approach might merit further investigation, something profound happened. There was a moment when everything fell into place. For a brief instant, on a very deep level, everything my friend said made complete sense. Sleep *is* whatever it *is*, and *does* whatever it *does*. It was *I* who'd been making sleep into a struggle — not sleep. A great sense of relief swept over me. Here was my answer.

By having no expectations of it, I could render sleep problem-free! Here was an insight I wanted to package and carry with me for the rest of my life. Without realizing it, my mind had instantly reverted to its old ways: I was again thinking about sleep as something to control, or at least influence, using The New Hands-Off Plan. The more my brain kicked into high gear to map out my new strategy, the more my flash of understanding faded away. Try as I might to recapture it, I could not.

However, something felt fundamentally different. As we left the coffee shop in silence, my Buddhist friend sensed that I had glimpsed something extremely important and that I was struggling to fathom it. We both knew that this was neither a matter of him giving advice, nor of my following a set of instructions. The point was for me to see it all clearly once again, this time for more than just a split second.

On the following day I called in sick to my workplace. At the library, with a pile of books on Zen Buddhism stacked in front of me, I began my quest to recapture that insight. Most of what I found was too complicated and abstruse to be of real use, and nowhere in Zen literature could I find anything specifically about sleep. I was frustrated and looking for guidance out of sheer habit, while Zen kept telling me there was no such thing. Slowly it began to dawn on me what the authors were trying to convey. It was my responsibility to look closely at the true nature of my problem without any preconceptions: in the moment of seeing it clearly, there would be peace. If I wanted to understand sleep, then I must learn to view it accurately, without the obstructions of my emotions or intellect.

At first it was puzzling to read the Zen writers' discourse on "seeing clearly," a different way of understanding that was not intellectual or academic. All of it sounded so peculiar. If the true nature of sleep (or, for that matter, anything else) could not be captured with concepts or explanations, how else could it be understood? It surprised me to realize, for the first time, that there exists a deeper sense of truth outside of reason and the reasoning process itself. Words cannot describe it, yet this kind of understanding is possible.

Over the course of several months, I began to discover for myself the true nature of sleep. As my comfort level grew with allowing slumber to "be what it is and do what it does," the demands of my will and intellect to control it diminished. In fact, the more I rejected my conceptual explanations of sleep in favor of a direct experience of it, the easier sleep became.

Eventually it was possible to fully grasp what insomnia actually is: an unnecessary form of suffering originating from one's own efforts to obtain sleep. All insomniacs know this important fact on a gut level, even if they are unable to articulate it. Most realize that, if it were just possible to stop trying so hard, then sleep would come naturally. Yet relinquishing our efforts seems impossible when we're laboring under the burden of sleepless nights. Our very nature is to struggle for whatever we believe we need, and, inevitably, the answer is Get More Sleep, a single-minded objective that takes on a life of its own. In the process, we lay our own trap.

The way out of this trap begins with an understanding of why we struggle in the first place. How the mind really works, and, moreover, how to accept its ways, are things that must be learned. Zen Buddhism offers us a framework for that undertaking.

And this is only half of the picture. The other half is slumber, of course, which reveals herself only to those with clear vision, unobstructed by the mind's frantic attempts to capture her. My own realization of this mysterious correspondence came after suddenly comprehending some of the key aspects of sleep; these will be discussed in subsequent chapters. Why didn't I notice these facets of sleep before? Because I was too busy *thinking!* The light comes on when the mind quiets down. This is the path to enlightenment.

The possibility of writing a book to chronicle my own path towards sleep-enlightenment never occurred to me in those early days of my journey. My priority was simply to understand my own sleep on a level that made it less troublesome. Because this path is essentially one where the mind is quiet, there is no opportunity to actually document anything. How does one describe the nature of sleep without employing the intellect's version of it? It's like trying to use words to describe van Gogh's "Starry Night," when it really must be *seen* to be appreciated.

Later, though, I felt compelled to share what I'd discovered, and therein lay my challenge: how could I describe something that exists outside of words and concepts? If sleep were some *thing* that could easily be defined and put into practice, there would be no problem in the first place. Slumber would have been rendered problem-free long ago. But the real nature of sleep makes this a completely different game. Therefore, if it was not going to be possible for me to recount the true nature of sleep, then perhaps I could at least record the discoveries I made along the way. But could they be understood by others? And finally, my path will not be the same as another individual's path: I had to realize and accept that what works for me might not necessarily work for others.

To uncritically assume that I could somehow light the way for others on the path to sleep-enlightenment felt not only egotistical, but also risky. A Zen approach is about experiencing reality free from any distortions; that is what gradually taught me to experience sleep on its own terms. My attempt to show others the true nature of sleep could only influence and thereby distort their own understanding. They might be distracted from their own experience by what I wrote, or immediately try to formulate a strategy from it, as I had initially done — in other words, never really look for themselves.

I have concluded that, in order to assist others in understanding their sleep problems as I have understood my own, my task must be limited to helping quiet the intellect and removing any barriers that obstruct the precise observation of the mind. Such an endeavor cannot be a book about me — it must be a book about you. Or more precisely, what you the reader believe about sleep, perhaps in ways that obscure its true nature. That is what this rather modest little book is all about.

To the extent that self-knowledge is at the heart of Zen, some of what is explored in these pages has less to do with sleep and more to do with Zen. This is not an intentional expansion of the subject matter, but simply a necessary part of the process: if the goal is to see sleep clearly on its own terms, then we must learn the art of seeing. That is what Zen is trying to tell us.

Of course, this approach can be used to address other problems and concerns, but for the purposes of this book, the application of Zen is mainly limited to the topic of sleep. Perhaps I will have whetted your appetite for more of this practice as it might relate to other problems or even to the Big Questions in life. There are numerous books available that treat Zen Buddhism more comprehensively, and with far more skill and insight than I have done here. Simply check your local bookstore or library.

✳

How to Use This Book

It's important to not expect that anything "new" — at least intellectually — will be revealed in a Zen approach. Our Western self-help literature teaches us to "add skills," "internalize explanations," "grasp key concepts." Such cognitive creations only take up space and require mental effort. Because academic knowledge is ever increasing, we have been led to believe that understanding consists of adding knowledge rather than removing it. Or, if nothing is added, then we must at least replace or update it. Not here. Enlightenment transcends academics and "knowledge about..." — especially in the case under consideration, our knowledge about sleep.

The "enlightenment" depicted here is not just a matter of belief, as it is in other (especially Western) traditions and philosophies. To get the most out of this book, it will be necessary for you to take the time to search for the inmost meanings of the words used here, and set aside what you may automatically think they mean. In a rather simplistic nutshell:

Read the words. Search to find what the words refer to, whether they are pointing to your own assumptions or to a particular aspect of sleep. Compare what you *see* with what you *think*.

You won't find an outline of step-by-step, easy-to-follow instructions to "a better night's sleep tonight!" as you might in a more conventional self-help book. The process of discovery in this book takes us on a journey that spirals inward, with themes introduced and then recurring, their meaning becoming clearer as understanding grows. Some Zen teachers say that all they do is repeat the same thing to their students, over and over, in different ways. A similar process is involved here: all of these words refer to a single shift in understanding — a shift so subtle that it may require many different promptings before it is apprehended by our normal consciousness.

So the best approach to take is simply one that goes with the flow. Consider this a road trip, where you encounter the unexpected and have the luxury of spending as much or as little time as you want at each attraction. Something particularly mysterious or enjoyable? Spend more time there. If you want to backtrack, feel free.

That said, you may feel an urge to flip ahead: however, the actual process of removing layers of misunderstanding about sleep is more easily accomplished if you first read this book cover to cover. In fact, I advise you to not proceed unless the issue at hand is well understood. In Zen, removing mental obstructions that cloud our vision is paramount: if we conduct our first, more basic observations as deeply and thoroughly as we can, the later, more difficult ones will be more penetrable.

Don't expect instant enlightenment, of course. Glimpsing reality through the fog of thinking takes time and practice. Often it requires repeatedly returning to earlier points that you assumed were understood. Thus, what might appear to be the useless repetition of a particular theme in a more conventional book has, in fact, an important purpose in this one.

Along the way, you'll encounter terms referring to different aspects of your self. While easily interchangeable, these words do carry subtle differences in meaning. "Consciousness" refers to the broadest sensation of oneself and one's surroundings, a kind of ongoing organic perception of our lives in our bodies and in the larger environment. "Awareness," on the other hand, refers to our more specific sense of events in our environment — both outer and inner — and which often drifts about without our intention. For instance, I'm aware now of the touch of my hands on this book, a slight headache, now the feeling of my back on the chair, and now the sounds outside the window. "Attentiveness" is a more intentionally focused form of awareness, like the attention you are giving to these words. It too can be directed outward or inward.

In this book, the term "mind" is used somewhat generically, referring to the part of our being that separates and categorizes all experiences. The "intellect" builds upon these divisions, creating a web of concepts and strategies. Finally, we'll refer most often to "the Thinker" (though usually not in very flattering terms), who generates all these different varieties of brain power.

Holding on to all this terminology as you read is not as important as sensing the meaning from the context. In this way, *Zen Sleep* is like a compass, pointing in the direction that you need to travel. If, out of habit, you keep your gaze focused on the compass, reading as though the words themselves are what are important, then you'll have gone nowhere. After all, these words are just ink spots on paper. What really matters is what you see and experience, beyond the reach of any book.

To facilitate this, you'll find a few questions to consider at the end of each chapter. They are called "observations," because they aren't exercises per se. Rather, these open-ended inquiries offer you the opportunity to reflect on what you've read and perhaps apply the material to your own life. Since self-dialogue is an important part of personal growth, these suggestions will open up important avenues. So grab a cup of coffee (decaf, if you prefer!) and make yourself comfortable. Let's start with the obvious: why Zen?

❈

Chapter 1

Why Zen?

Sleep has, for many of us, become mysterious and prob-lematic. Despite our best efforts to control this part of our lives, night is often a time of dread when we're unable to sleep. Insomniacs long to be free from the confusion and anx-iety associated with what should be a pleasurable and rejuve-nating experience. There may be a realization that one's own mind contributes to the unrest, but no easy solutions exist. Root causes are nowhere to be found.

The high rate of visits to doctors and sleep clinics, abuse of medications, and frequent media coverage indicate that the problem of insomnia is getting worse in the general pop-ulation. When the usual methods don't work, it makes sense to look for others, and that is the point at which we now find ourselves in regard to sleep. On this matter, neither religion nor science, the two dominant ways of interpreting the world, have much to offer in the way of meaningful help.

Mainstream religion rarely addresses the subject of insomnia directly. There is general spiritual support in the form of prayer, which is used to address a wide range of human suffering. For the most part, sleepless nights are treated like any other troublesome part of life, and addressed within the conventions of a particular faith. Some schools of New Age thought occasionally speak to the issue of sleep, but only to theorize that dreams are actually journeys to other realms, or other unprofitable beliefs. There exists no specific religious ritual that has been proven to aid those in need of sleep.

Science has offered considerably more assistance to some insomniacs, though not with complete success. Medical science treats sleep like any other biological function, and to some degree it can succeed in inducing or delaying sleep with medication. This is not to say that anything has been resolved. What has evolved is a sleep science like that associated with manageable illnesses such as diabetes: symptoms may be mitigated, but the underlying causes remain. A whole chapter is dedicated to sleep science later on in this book.

Nonmedical treatments for insomnia, like those offered by psychology, usually suggest environmental or attitudinal adjustments. Clinical psychology leads the way in this arena, with exhortations to change your life and take control of your problems. It would tell us that if we first clarify what our problems are — inner or outer, past, present, or anticipated ones — and then systematically resolve them, stresses and tensions will dissolve and our insomnia (and other troubles) will be fixed. Other schools of psychology teach clients to rethink their conflicts, and to find new ways of thinking about things in general. But, as we may know all too well, sleep can be particularly resistant to efforts to control it — and it usually couldn't care less what the experts have to say about it.

Likewise, sleep has a way of doing its own thing when the focus is turned toward the bedroom. Purchasing a new mattress, hiding the alarm clock, listening to soft music or sounds of nature, etc., are all attempts to alter the environment. No one strategy, alone or in unison with other changes, has shown itself to significantly aid those in need of rest. Yet we feel compelled to continue our efforts to capture sleep by making adjustments, whether internal or external.

Forcing change is a tradition in Western culture, and the fact that Zen requires no behavioral or cognitive change is problematic for a Western mind. "After all," the usual thinking goes, "if there is suffering then there must be a cause, and when we remove or modify that cause, the suffering will go away."

So in picking up this book for the first time, you most likely wondered, "What kind of solutions does Zen provide?" Your assumption might be that, since Zen is a particular philosophy, it must have a unique "spin" on sleep. In reality, Zen is about removing *all* manner of interpretation in order to replace our concepts with direct experience. Sleep is just one of the many things we fail to understand because the mind always has its own explanation — and that explanation is not the real thing. To attempt to answer the question "Why Zen?" is to clog the mind with yet another version of reality, to reinforce the Thinker's perspective: "It's only a matter of finding the 'right' way." But there is no right way: there is only how things *are*, which can rarely if ever be captured by a set of beliefs. How things really are is what Zen reveals.

Your intellect, which we are calling the Thinker, will struggle with this. It wants Zen to have its own rationale, beliefs, and practices. And Buddhism can provide rituals and intellectual byways that are able to accommodate the Thinker. However, in Buddhist traditions as in most others, these accommodations mostly act as distractions. There is no particular pathway to sleep espoused by Zen. So don't be afraid — allow your mind to protest.

We begin our journey not by surrendering to the Thinker, or fleeing from it, but by seeing beyond it. A more important question to ask than "Why Zen?," which appeals to the intellect, might be "Why not Zen?" "Why Zen?" asks Zen to justify itself with arguments and rationales, and to appease academic types, this chapter will address the advantages of Zen as well as the failures of conventional approaches to the problem of insomnia. The more reflective query, "Why not Zen?," digs much deeper, confronting the Thinker's usual strategies, challenging it to prove that its ways are better — or not. Asking "Why not Zen?" forces us to justify *non*-Zen methods of dealing with sleep problems, and our hitherto unexamined beliefs about sleep will finally see the light of day.

Therein lies our freedom, because we will discover that intellect-based explanations of sleep have but a flimsy basis in reality. We will discover that anything not-Zen, which is to say everything we *think* we know about sleep, is of questionable value. There may be much to occupy the mind, but none of it will cure our problem with sleep.

Alas, the Thinker will not loosen its grip until this becomes crystal clear. When our thought-full conceptions of sleep finally crumble under intense examination, we will be freed from our false understandings of this issue. What remains is the true nature of slumber, to simply be experienced rather than explained. Therein lies our game plan.

Beyond the usual

Zen says that suffering is actually a result of the "usual thinking" we employ to explain and control our day-to-day experiences. In fact, *any* thinking, no matter how nontraditional, will only block the path to true understanding. Why? Put in the most fundamental terms, it's because there is far more to our existence than the reasoning process can grasp. We are a part of the universe, which is a vast and constantly evolving flow of energy, every moment giving birth to the next. The Thinker likes a beginning, a middle, an end, and a tidy summary: our universe provides far too much unfolding information for the Thinker to process. A system of complex continuity can only be intuited with direct, moment-to-moment awareness of its continually changing contours. In this way, the potential exists for sleep to be experienced naturally, in the moment it arrives and as it unfolds — just as we could experience every other moment throughout the day and throughout our lives — rather than analyzing it all with the mind. Directly experiencing the flow of reality gives us a more complete understanding than do the mind's stale recollections and groundless projections.

A clear vision of sleep is free from any attempt to encapsulate or analyze it. This is a type of understanding that exists on a different level than academic knowledge: it requires us to be in sync with the flow of the universe, without regard to the "how" and "why" of it. Right now this may seem too abstract, but that's because quiet reflection on the nature of things plays no role in contemporary Western culture. Yet this is exactly the approach needed for understanding slumber. The anguish of sleepless nights, barring the presence of an underlying medical condition, is for the most part the result of the Thinker's relentless need to analyze and control experience, rather than merely being present *with* it. Or so a Zen master would say. Surely this possibility deserves investigation.

The duty to sleep

One of the most common ways that the mind creates sleep-lessness goes unnoticed: that is, the widespread tendency to place enormous significance on sleep. We do this without knowing why we do it, let alone what its consequences may be. Many, in fact, feel that they have a "duty" to sleep. In reality, it is simply the dominant social standard to set aside time after sundown for rest. If it seems odd to be regarding sleep in an abstract social context, it's because we aren't used to examining the influence that social norms and assumptions have on our view of our common day-to-day experiences. We aren't used to the self-examination required by Zen.

Social customs are simply ways of organizing group behavior. Conforming to social customs regarding sleep is an option but not an obligation. Sleeping, whether done alone or with others, is essentially a solitary experience: it is not required for anyone else's well being but our own. To attach a sense of duty to something that has no impact on others makes no sense. We may feel an obligation to sleep because of a vague apprehension that a lack of alertness during the day might have some kind of negative impact on our lives. If you look closely, though, you'll see that it's not the amount of sleep we get that really affects us — it's our expectations of how others might react the next day that make us anxious. We'll examine this particular misconception more thoroughly later in this book. For now, just recognize that sleepy feelings do not an obligation make. We humans have a propensity for missing the significance of truly important connections because we are anxiously looking in the wrong place. So warned the Buddha.

Discovering that there is no duty to sleep can bring comfort to those who have subconsciously believed otherwise. This is just a start, however: more sleep-enlightenment is possible, provided we can identify and examine other spurious assumptions and test their validity against direct experience.

Sleep and success

If an employer wants an employee to be alert for their job, it isn't sleep per se that's at issue — it's job performance. Some people sleep very little and perform just fine at work. Albert Einstein, for example, never slept more than an hour or two at a time, but managed to do brilliant work all the same. On the other hand, some people sleep soundly all night and perform rather poorly at work. Clearly, it's our *performance* that matters, not the number of hours of sleep we get. Habit makes it difficult to give up our thought-based conjectures about what contributes to the successful outcome of human endeavors — even in the face of countless examples of sleepiness *not* impeding success, and even more examples of abject failure despite absolute alertness.

We're beginning to uncover evidence to contradict the deeply held belief that a good night's rest is necessary for success the next day. Could it be that rest (which, by definition, involves no activity) is less important than other factors — our level of skill and interest, along with situational specifics — that create our experience of what constitutes a successful daily life? This is difficult to comprehend when sleep is customarily given so much weight. If anything that happens during the day has a relationship with the previous night's sleep, it's an assumed one, however obvious it may be to the Thinker with its continual need to "figure it out." Can you see this presumed connection with your eyes or touch it with your finger? Is there some way, through direct experience instead of analysis, to confirm that such a correlation exists? If not, then how do you know it's there?

The Thinker *believes* it is there because rest seems to bring alertness, and alertness seems to be a condition for success. But are either sleep or alertness necessary for success? A Zen master would tell us to ignore the mind; observe things for yourself. Look closely to see if alertness — which you can directly experience in yourself — occurs frequently with success or not. What is *really* a necessary condition for success to occur? We can observe that sleep usually, but not always, precedes alertness and that alertness sometimes, but not always, precedes success. Can we really infer causality here? Or are alertness and success merely occurring in chronological order?

More importantly: what exactly *is* success? If we strip away our usual mental associations and emotional reactions to the word itself, "success" (or the lack of it) is merely a human judgment about whether particular desired goals were met or not. The drama of planning, desires, and disappointments exists not in the real world, but in the mind. To someone struggling to climb the corporate ladder, the idea of success is as real as a mountaintop, yet, in fact, it's not real at all. Zen points out the hazards of this kind of thinking.

The Buddha said that observing the way things change will give us a more accurate view of reality than the static concepts of the intellect. Did he mean to imply that concepts are not reality? In other words, that human conventions like "necessity," "importance," and "success" aren't really *real?* Well — yes. Close observation reveals that they can't be seen, touched, or otherwise verified, and that the meanings we give them tend to vanish, reappear, and change shape before our eyes. Constructs like these are born from the mind's desire to interpret and control the phenomena around us, and do not physically exist — no more than the little green men from Mars. Do we need any more proof that "necessity," "importance," and "success" aren't real? If something in our daily life can't be verified through direct experience, does it really deserve to be called Real? With the status quo so embattled, the Thinker is protesting mightily: its domain begins to be threatened when we first discover that our "Sleep is necessary for success" formula expresses nothing more than a customary belief.

Looking closely, we observe that our assumptions them-selves change depending upon when we start and stop notic-ing the sequence of things. If daytime success always seemed to come *before* restful nighttime slumber, would that mean that daytime success is necessary in order to sleep soundly? What is the difference between that misinterpretation, and the more common misinterpretation that begins its observa-tion at the end of the day and concludes that nighttime rest is necessary for daytime success?

The difference is that one — "success is necessary for sleep" — hasn't been much considered, and so has not taken hold in the culturally conditioned mind, while the other — "sleep is necessary for success" — is so deeply rooted as to be taken for granted. The two assumptions could be identical, except that they've been measured from arbitrarily selected points in time. Neither one is a particularly accurate view, since reality guarantees that things will always change from moment to moment.

To conclude: we can say that daytime success is *not* nec-essary for nighttime rest, because our direct experience has often shown us that rest often comes even when daytime activities haven't been particularly successful. And it's equally true to conclude that nighttime rest is not necessary for day-time success, because our experience has been that success has often come even when nighttime was not particularly restful. That is how it really happens, the Thinker and its beliefs notwithstanding. Are you beginning to see how it works?

Such mental aerobics are not intended for our entertainment, but rather to illuminate our problem. We may *believe* that sleep is necessary for success because of the way we look at it: that is, the way the mind looks at it. More devastating (to the Thinker) is that the way the mind sees things is often not even verifiable as real! By now the mind may be screaming in dissent, and loudness is its forte. But you don't have to give in: better to get used to it. Later on, we'll explore how to manage a defrocked intellect.

Out of the box

For the next few days, observe the evolving quality of the following sequence closely, without thinking about or analyzing it: "awake" evolves to "sleepy" and to "sleep," which shifts to alertness and back again, one thing leading to another. This is what Buddha referred to when he said that observation of change gives us an accurate picture of reality. But what exactly is it that we're looking for in this sequence? We're beginning to observe the mutable nature of consciousness: the mind wants to intrude into this flow, labeling some sensations with the word "alertness" and others with the word "sleep." If we can refrain from this habitual labeling during our observation, we'll have our first significant clue that these states may not be separate events after all, but different manifestations of the same thing — consciousness.

Our momentary glimpse of the changing nature of awareness has already opened a new door, but it's still too early to enter. Seeing the whole instead of its parts is a profound shift. It takes time. Keep in mind just how out-of-the-box this new way of looking at consciousness really is.

Freeing ourselves from self-imposed conceptual boundaries (like "necessity" and "importance") is crucial if we are to see the whole picture. Our mental frameworks, which perpetuate the illusion of parts, may seem to give us a measure of security. In the end, however, our ability to accurately perceive the subject at hand is clouded. Therefore, the challenge is not to "obtain" sleep per se, but to escape from how we *perceive* sleep.

Individuals vary widely when it comes to their ability to identify and set aside their cognitive beliefs. The more a particular idea has been reinforced by others, such as sleep's "importance," the harder it is to question it. We may have emotional investments in certain of our opinions, and some ideas may be connected to others in a kind of domino arrangement so that when one falls, the others topple, too. Our emotional need for stability may seem to preclude honest self-reflection. But the opportunity for insight still exists: we have an abundance of opportunities and plenty of time to test our beliefs against direct experience. The personal journey into sleep-enlightenment is more a one-step-forward, two-steps-back process — way back to the long-forgotten state of mind that existed before sleep was a problem. Zen does not offer a ten-step program to achieve good sleep, or anything else for that matter. But when you master its logic, new directions and insights are possible.

The shape of Zen

A Zen approach requires no background or skill. There are no prerequisites for self-examination, a practice that Buddhists have done for centuries. But self-examination lies largely outside the Western cultural model, which defines knowledge as derived from the external world, not originating inside oneself. Religious salvation or liberation have usually been construed as being achieved through personal accomplishment or the intervention of a transcendent deity. Therefore, Westerners who are unfamiliar with Eastern philosophy may believe Buddhism in general and Zen in particular to be enigmatic or inaccessible. Some pundits have indeed complicated our understanding of Zen with references to the cryptic riddles of the Zen masters, and multiple schools of interpretation. But, fundamentally, Zen is quite simple.

Zen is focused on discovering how your own mind creates unnecessary suffering. This is also a primary goal of clinical psychology, and in some respects they overlap. But Zen offers no analysis or method for seeing how one's mind operates: it teaches clear seeing and little else. The resulting disappearance of incorrect beliefs and accompanying suffering is merely a consequence of this unhindered vision.

Some say that Zen's continual scrutiny of the mind can become a counterproductive obsession with suffering, yet we do need to uncover the everyday messes that we have devised for ourselves. From the point of view that trouble is best dealt with by denial or avoidance, the examination of suffering could appear unhealthy: if focusing elsewhere means misery is more easily endured, why not? For the simple reason that our miseries will still exist, and one way or another, they will continue to demand our attention in uncomfortable ways.

Another common misunderstanding of Zen is that it promotes an escape from everyday life because its focus is inward. In truth, it does quite the opposite: Zen requires an up-close examination of sometimes painful realities. Rather than being escapist, it is a here-and-now approach, challenging us to ask questions like, "What insight can I gain from directly experiencing this moment?" and "Where did I get this particular assumption?" and "What is the result of my holding this belief?" Zen asks for our willingness to look unflinchingly at how we distort our world, and to compare that with how the world actually is. It's a journey into understanding oneself, which may well be the most rational and sane endeavor we will ever undertake.

A Zen approach to insomnia is fundamentally rational. It is rational because Zen is not a religion: there is no deity or belief system involved. Zen requires no leap of faith. For societies like ours, anchored in Judeo-Christian traditions, the absence of doctrines can be unsettling, signaling a lack of credibility. We assume that anything of value to our individual growth must have some element of belief. There is no answer to that, except to say that Zen is not a faith-based philosophy: it suggests, in fact, that we examine faith and belief themselves. No framework exists to promote any particular beliefs. Thus, you will find no theory of sleep within these pages. Although the mind is discussed, Zen does not take up residence there, as many religions do. Contemporary Buddhists may adopt Asian modes of dress and behavior and spend time meditating and performing ceremonies involving unfamiliar postures, and foreign languages in an attempt to gain inner wisdom. But this kind of cultural posturing is quite unnecessary.

A Zen approach to sleep is also readily accessible. It requires no money or materials, and there are no scriptures to learn or skills to acquire. Ironically, this can make it especially difficult for a Western mind to credit, because we're taught to believe that wisdom is attained only through external efforts and issuing from some external source, replete with texts and ritual paraphernalia. If learning doesn't come from outside of us, then where *does* it come from? The Buddha said (and it bears repeating): "It comes from your own direct observation."

As a beginning step, simply verify for yourself that the "duty to sleep" and the importance you place on it are products of your mind's tendency to assume a dominant role; they are not actual things that you can directly verify. It may be the nature of the intellect to form concepts and theories, but is there any reason to place direct experience in a subordinate position? The Buddha said that a mind given free reign to jump on the conceptual bandwagon, without ever looking at reality itself, is a messy mind, and such a mind is bound to cause turmoil and suffering. Zen will challenge you to look at what you are doing and what the alternatives are, as we have already begun to do.

Sleep-enlightenment is entirely possible if you are willing to open your eyes. You don't need to suspend disbelief, as though you are reading fiction or watching a movie. Indeed, the ways you may already be thinking about sleep may require a healthy dose of skepticism. Do they accurately reflect your own experiences? Zen doesn't ask you to accept anything at face value: it asks you to test the waters of reality and see for yourself.

Don't dismiss the challenges presented here without first testing their validity; responsibility for your own sleep-enlightenment, after all, lies with you. It's all optional, of course, but the fact that you're reading this book indicates that you're on a quest. All of what you've read so far could very well be a bunch of hooey — and probably is, according to the Thinker. Yet beyond the veto of the rational mind lies something far more valuable: the real nature of things. Quietly observe the location of your awareness for a moment: what are you paying attention to right now? That may seem fairly easy, but it takes courage to stop thinking and start looking.

We are beginning to see that this approach to sleep has no formal structure: and, because there is no "path" per se —

other than your own individual path — there are no guide-posts. And because there are no stages, but rather a burrowing through our layers of thought, there can be no common yardstick of progress. We either see our own thoughts as they relate to a larger picture, then assess their validity, or we don't. Concepts such as "progress" and "success" don't belong in this endeavor. Sleep is not a contest.

This is different from suppressing, replacing, or changing our beliefs. We must become comfortable with the kind of intellectual emptiness that can result from rejecting a long-held perspective. Hundreds of wise people over the ages have told us that to be mistaken is the human condition: we are better off when we humbly acknowledge that and learn to live with it. While our cognitive world may feel slighted, our spiritual and intuitive world will grow richer as our insight develops.

In the largest sense, the strongest basis for a meaningful understanding of the human condition is unwavering self-knowledge. Knowledge obtained this way offers the scholarly world a purpose and context within which truly worthwhile progress is possible. When it's not informed by an understanding of the true nature of our being, factual knowledge serves no real purpose and often leads to harmful undertakings.

It's because we all have a working knowledge of hunger that, over time, people have learned to develop and share the skills needed to grow food so that others don't go hungry. Likewise, we've developed the technical knowledge to explain sleep physiologically, but few of us possess insights derived from direct experience of sleep which could be used to help others in need. That's because we've been looking for the wrong kind of knowledge. Slumber lies outside our ability to explain or control: we need the freedom to experience it naturally, free from the Thinker's hectoring voice. Zen offers that opportunity.

The heart of Zen

At the heart of Zen is the observation that life will always escape our mind's attempts to quantify and qualify it; reality just doesn't fit inside the limitations of the human mind. There's nothing inherently wrong about the way the intellect generates its beliefs, it's just that these constructs will always remain just what they are: ideas, not reality.

This doesn't mean that ideas serve no purpose. Concepts can be valuable and deserve respect — they are our best helpers with certain types of problem-solving. This concession might appear to contradict Zen's stated goal of freeing us from the Thinker's distortions. Not so. Just bear in mind that the intellect's version of something is not the *only* version, and certainly not the most complete one. It's when we fail to see the forest for the trees that problems arise. An expert will tell you which tree is an elm, a birch, or a fir. And an expert will tell you their ages, and how the surrounding ecosystem has affected their growth. But an expert cannot give you the experience of the beautiful woods. Only you can do that.

Appreciating the beauty and magnificence of an ancient redwood tree is the kind of "seeing" that Zen is after. There exists an essence, a completely nonrational understanding of such a grand work of nature. One stands in awe, touching the bark that extends upward into the sky. It is *directly experienced,* free from any attempt by the mind to capture its nature with thoughts. A small child gazing at the redwood experiences the true nature of that tree far better than the most educated arborist whose mind is filled with facts and figures. The academic is blind while the child can see. The tree enlightens us with a meaning and depth far beyond the academic knowledge of the most comprehensive textbook on trees.

This is easy to understand: a description of an ancient redwood tree is a poor substitute for directly experiencing the real thing. (In fact it can *prevent* us from experiencing the real thing.) But it bears repeating: this does not make knowledge worthless. The Buddha talked extensively about becoming mind-free, but he never said to stop thinking completely. He simply said to be wary of what you think, examine your mind, and do not let it control you. Spend most of your time taking delight in the things around you by directly experiencing the moment.

This way of lucid perception, referred to so often here and in other books on Zen, can only be hinted at. No language

or method exists to capture it with words. "Seeing" reality is not exactly a matter of over-emphasizing our physical senses — although that can be one aspect of it. "Seeing" happens in that moment when a vital connection to everything in the whole situation is felt, making it utterly transparent and eminently workable. This book is an attempt to point the way to that dynamic perception in the realm of what we call sleep.

✴

Observations

✳ Identify any assumptions you had about Zen before picking up this book. Have they changed?

✳ Notice how you go about the process of self-examination. What feelings and/or thoughts come up?

✳ Determine if you, in general, value thinking about things over having a direct experience of them. Which do you trust more? Which do you appreciate more?

✳ Assess the degree of importance you place on sleep.

Chapter 2

Looking at Sleep

Having glimpsed the potential of what might lie beyond the reasoning mind, hopefully we are encouraged to keep looking. The Buddha's wisdom came from his realization that it was the mind that blinded him to reality, and the fact that the whole picture is not readily apparent to us now indicates that something is clouding our vision. Before a clearer picture of sleep's true nature can emerge, we must understand the intellect and other forces that have influenced us. This isn't an attempt to completely obliterate how our minds view sleep; rather, like the Buddha, we want to uncover our personal beliefs about sleep so as to not be blinded by them.

Cultural views of sleep

Our culture treats sleep as though it's a fairly straightforward phenomenon. Sleep is assigned a particular time, usually night, and a particular place, normally the bedroom. One thing that the Culture of Sleep particularly avoids is the key question of why we need sleep at all, because there is no easy answer. Beyond polite references, like "How did you sleep?," few people discuss the mysterious nature of slumber. Should we continue to pretend that we understand sleep? Perhaps, if one is sleepy, then sleep "makes sense." But when we cannot sleep, we're returned to the question of why we sleep in the first place.

The intellect can become demanding on this point, which presents a problem: we just don't have the kind of information that would satisfy the Thinker. As a species, we strive to understand our existence, and when something as ordinary as sleep fails to succumb to our investigations, perplexity ensues. It may be, however, that a less-than-perfect relationship with sleep is not only natural, but inevitable.

It's not socially acceptable to admit that our experience of sleep might be frightening, although not wanting to lose control is perfectly understandable. For some, striving to remain conscious makes far more sense than willingly giving up control. In this sense, the phenomenon we call insomnia is perhaps just a protective assertion against the loss of consciousness. Such a response could be seen as perfectly natural, rather than as a disorder of some kind. If you find yourself rebelling against the approach of sleepiness, why not appreciate that? Protecting the sovereignty of your awareness could be a good thing. For now, give yourself permission to rebel against sleep: the issues of control, choice, and responsibility will be explored more thoroughly later in this book.

Unfortunately, the term "insomnia" carries a negative value judgment. Our society bestows approval on the nightly act of going to bed and submission to sleep. Sleep is the goal, the Good, and the desire to remain awake and conscious at night earns a measure of disapproval. This is a carryover from a time when, as children, we were expected to be good little boys and girls who go right to sleep at the appropriate time. This expectation is no longer verbalized to adults, but the social and psychological vestiges remain.

Still, sleep arrives or not on its own schedule. Usually it comes in the evening, as expected. When sleep happens outside the culturally prescribed time, taking us by surprise, we are said to "nod off." Or, if we consciously permit ourselves to sleep during the day, we call it a "nap." Whatever labels we choose, it makes little sense to create a set of social values about something over which we have little control. The only things we *can* control when it comes to sleep are our responses to it and the meanings we assign it. Coloring sleep's arrival with the hues of morality serves only to muddle our understanding. There is no "should" or "shouldn't" — yet the expectation to surrender on cue still exists.

There are also hidden social meanings attributed to the state we call "sleepy." If it's the result of having been awake too long, we say that sleep is needed and the individual should go to bed. Or it might be that our sleepiness results from having already enjoyed the natural state of slumber for a long time, and wishing for it to continue as long as possible. Such idleness is often disapproved of, and we say that the individual has slept too much: they should wake up, get those chores done! Each admonition carries with it a message for the individual to somehow take responsibility for their state of consciousness.

This message to take control implies that there's a "right" amount of sleep to be had. It also implies that one can easily begin to sleep if necessary, or quickly wake up if one has had enough. And it suggests that being in some middle state between slumber and full wakefulness is not a legitimate place to be. Most importantly, it reinforces the notion that sleep is an *action* that one has control over, and that perhaps *ability* is somehow involved. But the only real decision involved is whether or not to accommodate sleep when it comes.

Yet sleep is not like other social imperatives. To even call sleep a "demand" is somewhat misleading, because sleep doesn't ask you to *do* anything. But it can be so adamant in its request for you to *stop* everything that it almost feels like a demand . . . and not all of us find it easy to oblige.

The invitation to sleep

Not everyone wants to accept sleep's invitation. After all, there may be better things to do than lose awareness of the external world and enter another realm. For some insomniacs, the whole process can be frightening: no longer surrounded by what is familiar, the onset of sleep means not knowing what is to come. Those who surrender are not necessarily smarter than those who don't. Perhaps, like newborns, they simply don't know any better.

For those who have trouble with sleep, the ideal world would be one where this uninvited visitor never knocks at the door. Imagine the extra time we'd have for ourselves, how much more could be accomplished if the boundaries between day and night were allowed to blur. And more importantly, there would no longer be a struggle every night.

Someone may say they "want" sleep, but that's because this visitor is *making them sleepy.* When we say that we "crave" sleep, what are we really saying? Perhaps only that we want to surrender to sleep instead of making the effort to resist it. Or maybe we want not to sleep but to escape consciousness. Often people who are depressed have a particularly good relationship with sleep because awareness is too painful — they happily abandon themselves. Others sometimes prefer to float halfway between slumber and waking, with no particular desire to be elsewhere.

If your soul could speak, it would probably say something like this: "For a certain number of hours each night, I raise the white flag and succumb to another power that, in essence, reaches inside me and turns the switch to Off. I relinquish myself entirely and enter nothingness, except for the dreams that may remind me of my daytime world. I give up my present world of conscious awareness with the knowledge that in a short while I shall get it back again. That is my choice. That is my sweet surrender."

Meeting sleep's arrival like this, with a conscious decision, could be a good response for those of us who fear the loss of control that sleep suggests. As awareness diminishes, we could put aside our assumptions and fears and make a friendly connection. Just as it takes time for a new acquaintance to become a trusted friend, it can take time to become familiar and comfortable with the realm that exists naturally beneath all our cognitive fabrications.

The feeling of sleep

When sleepiness first appears as a diminishing of our awareness of the external world, why not find the pleasure in those feelings? This pleasure is an effortless one, very much like floating wherever the tide takes you. Yes, there's movement, but it's a movement that carries you, not one that forcibly pushes or pulls. You are merely along for the ride. Some people find actual physical movement to be sleep-inducing. Bus or train trips can be good venues for getting to know sleep.

For newborns, being rocked has a similar effect. Adults who want to learn to understand sleep — the natural state of freedom from a busy mind — must become comfortable with being moved just like an infant. This doesn't necessarily imply being rocked to sleep by another person; it does mean allowing something else to move you from one place to another. The next time you're on a road trip with a friend, excuse yourself to the back seat for a short nap. Whether sleep actually occurs or not doesn't matter; what does matter is the opportunity to relax while movement from here to there is done for you. Movement is no longer your responsibility. No demands intrude on your awareness, so it can safely drift away.

In fact, in sleep there are no demands at all. Sleep is like a return to a liquid womb where movement happens without accountability, with no need for explanations or excuses. No sound, no light, no activity. Sleep, unconsciousness, is the place you inhabited before you remember anything else, when all that existed was the Great Beyond. That experience is still there for us in sleep's embrace. Of all the places in the universe, none is more secure, inviting, and safe than this place. Sleep seeks you out to protect you, just like a mother's womb. It envelopes you in security, cradling you in a cocoon far removed from the world outside. This is how it *feels*.

Remembering sleep

Some people can remember their very early childhood years, when sleep was simple and natural. Choices were limited, and "personal empowerment" unknown. A good deal of early human life is spent sleeping. Sleep is our starting point; only later does awareness of the environment develop. Now is a good time to see if a memory of that original domain is buried somewhere in your psyche. See if you can remember and extend an open hand, because deep inside us there's a longing to trust. This need to simply *be,* free from the intrusions of the external world, takes us far beyond the domain of the Thinker. The "how" or "why" of it really doesn't matter. Sleep is a form of deliverance, as though we earn an escape from the daily task of survival — and we earn it every day! Sleep is our biological liberation from the stress of constant awareness.

On an intuitive level, letting go of the external world is an act of relinquishing control. People who surrender to sleep willingly do so because they know the pleasure it brings, and their response to sleep's invitation is effortless. For the rest of us, there's no hurry to get to that level of intuitive acceptance. We have a new opportunity every night to begin sensing the arrival of sleep and slowly exploring the potential for surrender.

In a sense, adults have to start over, relearning how to accommodate something that doesn't make sense intellectually. Because adults tend to cater to the intellect, if something

doesn't register mentally, it often doesn't register at all. How can you recognize "nothingness"? Newborns have nine months of practice at literally doing nothing; adults have untold years of enforced capitulation to everything modern society throws at us. Perhaps if one could escape civilization and live worry-free on an island paradise, then one could relearn how to sleep.

Most of us have experienced periods in our lives when we found ourselves sleeping effortlessly. Usually this occurred when there were no demands on our time, and we somehow found our way to a place of deep peace. It might have happened on vacation, or perhaps a long weekend. Remembering what the luxury of that release felt like can be a sign of what to look for when we're searching for a grounding in sleep.

Unfortunately, few of us enjoy a continuous vacation; day-to-day existence is much more challenging. If many of the demands on us are adversarial in nature, then we tend to look upon sudden changes in awareness (like "falling" asleep) in the same way. But unlike a client or colleague, slumber cannot be convinced to take less than what it's asking for. It wants it all — at least that's how the Thinker sees it. Sleep is something that will keep coming around for more until it claims all of your awareness. If you offer it something less than full submission, sleep will only continue to pester you.

Relating to sleep

Sleep can be like a relentless mosquito that keeps buzzing around until it finally gets its fill of blood, then flies off. If you brush it away, it keeps coming back. If you let it take what it wants, it will leave you alone, but only for a while. Eventually it will come back for more of the same.

Those who enjoyably submit to sleep might shudder at such an unpleasant analogy. However, this is not written for those individuals, but for the rest of us who encounter sleep with even more dread than we might a nagging mosquito. Because no long-lasting sleep-repellent exists, sleep-avoiders must somehow come to terms with allowing this uninvited guest to feast on our awareness.

If you've ever had a mosquito land on your skin and begin its work, you are immediately confronted with choices — not only whether to allow the mosquito to proceed, but also choices about your mental and emotional reactions. If you believe a mosquito bite is deadly, then fear will overcome you. That's the Thinker (and its companion, emotional reactivity) doing its job.

It's the Thinker who perceives sleep as something separate from itself, like a raiding mosquito. Would the Buddha have worried about slumber stealing his consciousness? Quite the contrary: the Buddha saw that sleep is nothing but another form of consciousness, so there is nothing to be taken away. Can you point to or directly experience that which is "taken away" by sleep, and that which does the taking? The larger picture will gradually reveal itself, so be patient.

How each of us responds to sleep reflects our own particular relationship with it. We spend far more time examining our relationships with other people, yet sleep is a life-long relationship that surely deserves the same careful attention. At the beginning of life, we seem to have had the best possible relationship with this companion. What went wrong?

In fact, there is no "right" or "wrong" way to relate to sleep. After all, we have the perfect right to approach our relationships with others in uniquely different ways. From the Zen point of view, the ideal relationship is one that respects the true nature of each party; therefore, cultivating a positive relationship with sleep means permitting it to be whatever it is. And this certainly isn't a question of skill. To sleep like a baby is indeed to have a very accommodating relationship with sleep, and babies are usually not considered more skillful than adults. Maybe we've simply become too busy as adults to maintain a trusting relationship with this part of life.

Too often, we approach the arrival of sleep the same way we approach a person whom we're unsure about, with caution and one eye on the door. This might be normal behavior with regard to an unknown visitor, but it is counterproductive when it comes to sleep. Trust has to be an inherent part of this relationship. There can be no search for power, no maneuvering to gain the upper hand that characterizes so many human relationships. Constantly strategizing in an attempt to control "the other" precludes any possibility of allowing oneself to be vulnerable — which plainly doesn't work with sleep.

Sleep in modern life

We must also integrate sleep into a day-to-day existence that has, for most of us, become unsuitable for rest and relaxation. Modern life is full of demands, triggering that mechanism which keeps us awake and alert. If we only needed to be awake for primitive natural activities, there would be less of a problem. Now we find ourselves stuck in a kind of adaptational wakefulness, continuously responding to a level of demand for which we have not evolved.

This is not to say that, given the opportunity, an individual would do nothing but sleep, only waking to fulfill a few needs. But such a lucky individual would certainly find it much easier to escape the many influences that stimulate our wakefulness. Students of Zen pay close attention to what they actually do, moment to moment, during the course of a day. Inevitably, they find that much of a routine day is spent dealing with unimportant matters, material things, and assorted responsibilities. While some of our affairs certainly seem pressing, and may be for financial reasons, much of it is just insignificant noise. Acknowledging this often helps to lighten the load, relieving the pressure we feel to stay focused on the many details of daily life.

There is also the impact of our commercial culture to consider. In the West, creating desires and satisfying them has, for economic reasons, become the dominant activity and therefore the primary point of reference for how many of us think. Living inside this framework of manufacturing and then satisfying cravings, we unconsciously conclude that sleep is like every other need so eloquently detailed in advertising. Pills, special bedding, therapy, and other methods are touted as ways to "buy sleep." If it works just a little, then more of the same is tried. The Buddha warned that when we feed our desires, they grow, creating an ever-expanding cycle that has no end. This continuous preoccupation with cravings and the ensuing struggle to fulfill them only hinders us in our quest for sleep's true nature. Sleep requires no craving or satisfaction of craving: there is only the invitation to relax and stop attending to the clutter that surrounds us.

Medical and sociological experts affirm that insomnia is on the rise precisely because of all of the clutter, and no one doubts that modern life has become stressful and complicated. On the surface, this argument certainly sounds plausible. But the *type* of stress we experience is, in fact, far less threatening than in the past. We certainly have a larger quantity of details to keep track of, and while this makes life more complicated, it doesn't necessarily make it more stressful. The pre-modern world was rife with famines, wars, plagues, invasions, and general anarchy, and dire poverty was the lot of most of humanity, yet nowhere is there mention of widespread insomnia. Given the relative ease of life today — compared with the struggle to survive that our predecessors endured — this seems contradictory. Shouldn't there be *less* insomnia today, not more?

How can we explain this paradox? As the Buddha would say: Just look. And if we look, we find that we've created and are inhabiting the Age of Information, completely blind to the consequences for our psyche. The Buddha discovered that our awareness tends to take on the qualities of whatever it is focused on — in other words, we become *what we give our attention to.* So, if forty hours per week are spent thinking instead of performing physical activities in the real world, guess what becomes the normal mode of our awareness? That's right, *thinking.* Analyzing. Conceptualizing. Add to this all the responsibilities of modern life, and we find that our consciousness has become distorted. Life is reduced to an overwhelming number of concepts, the modern currency of social and intellectual exchange. Sleep has been transformed into just another concept, one of many, ready to be processed, checked off the list and filed away in the morning, to be thought about again much later in the day (at the appropriate time, of course — nighttime). In short, reality has been hijacked by the Thinker. What a fine recipe for insomnia.

There must be some way that people of average means can cope, some way to turn off not the arrival of sleep but the realm of thoughts and ideas that demand so much attention and distort our experience of life. Perhaps we can't turn it off completely, but at least we can turn down the volume.

With a clearer view of our predicament, some small steps toward a less "mind-centric" way of living begin to emerge. One obvious measure is to mitigate those factors that require us to be hyper-alert and thinking. A change of employment or simplification of lifestyle may help. In other words, we can compromise and find a middle ground where the things that seem to urgently demand our mental attention are scaled down in significance, through changes in either our behavior or our perspective.

It's important to realize, however, that these kinds of answers are more like band-aids than real solutions, simply because it's impossible to return to an earlier time when cognitive "stuff" hadn't yet overtaken the real world of direct experience. Our real challenge is to find a way through the Thinker's maze of concepts to arrive at the kind of understanding of sleep possessed by earlier generations.

Our ancestors weren't detoured by one of this era's foremost roadmaps to sleep: sleep science. This particular distortion, institutionalized and widely viewed as the gospel truth, caters perfectly to the Thinker; science personifies the practice of emphasizing concepts over direct experience. This particular conceptual map, explored in the next chapter, has taken center stage, completely overriding our sense of where reality lives. Intellectually and emotionally, to be without this plan can be daunting. Yet only when we gather the courage to proceed without it, directly observing our actual moment-to-moment experience, will we be liberated from the obstructions to a clear understanding of sleep.

✳

Observations

✳ Look closely at how the culture (your upbringing, the media, etc.) have influenced your relationship to sleep. Identify your own "shoulds" and "should nots."

✳ Become aware of your personal reactions to sleep's arrival.

✳ Pay attention to the ways that modern life causes you to do an inordinate amount of thinking and reacting. Do you see any ways to mitigate that?

Chapter 3

The Science of Sleep

Prior to the advent of science, sleep apparently received little attention. While references to sleep problems can be found dating back to the seventeenth century, they are rare. Several early English poems alluded to dreams and the healing properties of sleep, and it was a common fear to be mistaken for dead when actually in a deep sleep. It was not until medical science had mapped out the human body and identified the functions of the organs that an attempt was made to fit slumber into the scientific paradigm. During the same period, medical doctors gradually began claiming the body and its processes as their exclusive domain, and lowly individuals were no longer considered qualified to understand or deal with their own problems. Finally, in the twentieth century, a working theory of sleep evolved, greatly aided by advances in the measurement of brain activity.

Once sleep was viewed as a bodily function, its absence was assumed to imply a disease process, comparable to the inability to eat or to eliminate waste. Yet before this scientific model of the physical self took hold, a day or two without sleep, food, or elimination was no particular cause for concern — or at least no one bothered to document that concern. Today, with the medical model of our bodies firmly implanted in our collective consciousness, a day or two with one bodily function or another slightly awry can cause considerable worry, maybe even a visit to the doctor. Our belief that "sleeplessness = illness" is so ingrained that it can take great courage to permit our consciousness to abide in whatever form it takes in a given moment, rather than assessing it through the lens of science.

With a newly identified "illness" in need of a name, the term *insomnia* (from the Latin) was coined and the race was on to find a cure. Of course, in order to do that it was first necessary to understand sleep.

Catch-22

Alas, the science of sleep was misguided from its inception. Researchers, realizing that they could never discover the *why* of sleep, have insisted on explaining it as an inherent — if incomprehensible — function of the body and brain. In compensation, they try to define in a physiological sense what constitutes "good sleep." This attempt resembles a linguistics professor trying to describe "good grammar" in a mysterious foreign language. Certain words and speech patterns are identified in subjects who speak the language well, analogous in this discussion to those who sleep soundly. Then that gold standard is used to judge subjects who *don't* speak the language well — all the rest of us, who are insomniacs. The result? Lots of charts and graphs.

Every possible measurement of bodily functions during sleep has been made in an effort to mechanically sum up the process. In addition to the usual vital signs taken when patients are awake, in sleep research there is an increased emphasis on brain waves, rapid eye movements, and leg twitching. From a physiological point of view, these measurements may hold some interest. However, those who fluently speak the language of sleep can't really teach it to others, and those who study it are merely attempting to quantify something that is fundamentally subjective.

After all, sleep is essentially down-time, when we experience cycles of diminished physical activity and consciousness. These changes are intrinsically personal and subjective, far richer and more nuanced than the reductionist viewpoint of science can reveal. The great mystery of sleep cannot fit into the narrow conceptual boundaries of "physiological process" the way that science has defined that term.

In fact, nothing of "sleep" actually exists to be measured by scientists except for a few limited physiological shifts that occur when consciousness changes its direction from wakefulness to sleep. And the functions being measured are the same ones that occur when we're awake — the only difference is that they are being assessed at a different point in time. So, in effect, what is actually being measured is not "sleep" at all, but relative changes in common body functions. Thanks to the influence of sleep science, our gaze is usually planted not on the experience of sleep itself, but fixed on the monitoring instruments that pick up minor and — to be honest — insignificant physiological signs of sleep.

The emphasis on measurement further reinforces the misunderstanding that sleep is somehow an entity in and of itself. Scientists will indicate someone sleeping and say, "That is sleep." Follow along and try this yourself. Become a scientist and point to someone sleeping (a picture of a person in bed with their eyes closed will suffice) and say out loud, "That is sleep." Carefully observe that there are only two things that can be verified through direct experience in this scenario. First of all, visual evidence shows us a person. That is all our eyes tell us; we don't really know what that person is actually doing — perhaps they're awake and merely resting their eyes. Secondly, you can observe your mind creating the idea of "sleep" from visual, cultural, and memory cues. Notice how that concept is drawn not from anything external or real, but from the mind's repertoire of associations and labels — and the label "sleep" is used to indicate a person lying down with their eyes closed. This particular word is laden with meanings

Birth of a concept

that have been accumulated over the years through collective assumptions and a medicalized culture, finally coming to signify that such a scene constitutes sleep, a separate and significantly different physiological state of being.

However, sleep *itself* can't be pointed to because sleep doesn't exist *except as a concept.* If it were more than just a concept, you could see an actual separate entity with your eyes and touch it with your finger. Instead, the Thinker creates this powerful set of ideas which acts like a magnet, pulling us in its own direction rather than towards the actual experience that lies beyond the reach of ideas. The scientific paradigm that science applies in an attempt to capture what we call "sleep" fails miserably, because the true experience lies outside the "mind-centric style" of recording reality. All the poor Thinker can do is work with the *idea* of sleep, most easily within the framework of science.

Likewise, the idea of "awake" exists solely in the mind. Try looking at "awake," touching it with a finger, or in some other way verifying that what we call "awake" is substantially more than just an idea. Yes, it is a particular form of consciousness, one that manifests a heightened awareness, which we *label* "awake." But nowhere is there a separate *thing.* See how the mind tricks us? Later on we will explore the tendency of mind to apply labels and divide everything up into opposites. For now, simply verify how the Thinker has hijacked the experience of consciousness with a design that obscures its true nature of one continuous flow that takes many forms.

This most fundamental observation — that "asleep," like "awake," does not exist except in our minds — challenges common sense. Wouldn't it be logical to draw the conclusion that this entire book is one big contradiction? Here's a book about sleep that claims there is no such thing! Well, from the Thinker's perspective, that might be true. If sleep doesn't really exist, why is so much written about it in these pages?

This apparent contradiction occurs because there are two kinds of perspectives on sleep. Only one can be written about — the *concept* of sleep — and that's the one that doesn't exist in the real world. It's immaterial, a mind-thing, and can't be directly verified; it's not reality. The other perspective — *how sleep really is* — arises directly from our individual experience, and can only be hinted at with words. It's the real thing, deeply felt and intensely personal. Alas, it's the first view that blocks our vision of the second, so our time is spent exploring the domain where sleep doesn't really reside.

But if we can get comfortable with the fact that reality isn't conceptual (which the Thinker demands), and that truth is often a matter of perspective, then many doors will open for us. It means that we are willing to acknowledge that anything of the intellect will, as the Buddha discovered, tend to lead us away from the real thing. We won't allow the Thinker to abort our journey just because paradoxes abound — we'll continue, and ultimately discover the path that is most useful.

When the going gets tough, it's time to return to the Buddha's central message, that real value lies in the direct experience of the present moment rather than what we think about with our intellect. The Thinker will insist that the shifts in physiological measurements which researchers so fondly record are the real thing — because that is what a mind does. Its business is to separate experience into opposites. If there is a thing called "awake," then there must be an opposite, "sleep," which must also be some *thing*.

Yet close examination reveals we misinterpret the various *labels* we give our consciousness as actual things themselves, never feeling the underlying continuity of how it all ebbs and flows in the first place. So instead of simply experiencing consciousness as it changes moment to moment, we invent fancy machinery to capture, and thereby make "real," the *label* we give those particular moments that has Thinker baffled. Such a mind-centric approach inevitably obscures the larger picture. Few of us observe our minds as intently as Zen practice requires, so this long excursion may seem like repetition—and that's precisely what happens when you really observe. You look again, and again, and again. And one thing we discover is that the attention showered upon a label we assign to a particular moment of consciousness is like shining a light into an academic black hole. Don't expect anything genuinely useful back. It's only a *label*.

If a scientific approach leads us nowhere, at least we have some indication of where *not* to go. Remember that our goal is the big picture, that clear vision that sees beyond the illusion of parts. Can we directly observe sleep and simply see it as a different form of wakefulness? No, not yet — the way is not yet completely cleared. The Thinker is still in the driver's seat.

After all, the experience of sleep exists, the intellect exclaims. It was only last night that sleep happened, right? Well, yes — the experience happened. Does that mean there is a separate entity at work, a thing that is *not you?* Close inspection reveals that *nothing separate* is there. The old way of looking at sleep — as something that comes to visit in order to take away something else called awareness — has fallen by the wayside. Those concepts may still exist in the mind, but they no longer have to override our own experience of consciousness: one continuous movement of our awareness towards and away from our surroundings.

To understand this is to glimpse reality. If a person were to tell the Buddha that they've experienced sleep, he would probably ask, "What exactly was experienced? If you can describe it with words, then you don't fully grasp its true nature." You are looking in the wrong place, hoodwinked by the Thinker.

This is not an outright rejection of medical science, but rather an acknowledgement that in Western society, intuitive understanding has been replaced by numbers. The mind's dualizing and dehumanizing tendencies run wild in the medical world, creating a model of healing based not on the body's own potentials but on the manipulation of biological measurements through chemicals and invasive procedures. When everything is reduced to parts and figures, the medical doctors can claim our bodies as their province. No longer do we feel empowered to help ourselves, even in the profoundly personal domain of our own consciousness.

Looking in all the wrong places

Brain waves, eye and muscle movements, respiration — all the physiological indicators that sleep researchers so diligently measure — also occur during the waking state. So "sleep versus waking" is really a matter of degree: when measurements indicate a certain magnitude of change, then "sleep" is said to be achieved. Of course nothing is really "achieved," because sleep is not something to accomplish. All that we get from the process of measuring physiological changes is just that — a measurement. Attempting to quantify reality is not the same as understanding its nature. The reduction in physiological activity from the point of full wakefulness to the point where we begin to talk of "sleep" will always lack a scientific explanation. Sleep science hasn't even come close to answering our original question: Why does a transition from the waking state to the sleep state occur at all? We know that without this change, a person persisting in the waking state will slowly lose the ability to function over a period of several days. But why? If we attempt a linear approach to these questions, we find ourselves going around in circles, the result of our need to explain sleep logically. The Thinker is still in charge.

Sleep must be a bodily function, we tell ourselves. But what kind of function is it? Digestion brings nutrients to cells. Elimination removes waste from the body. Perspiration cools the body. And sleep... what? Renews the mind? This seems glib and inadequate. We know that we need sleep, but what for?

The simplest answer is that we need sleep because we get sleepy. To one who effortlessly moves in and out of slumber, this is sufficient — but that person would probably not be reading this book. The rest of us still need to rid ourselves of our roadmaps, so it will be helpful to uncover the questionable connection between biology and sleep.

Sleep medicine

Few of us reflect on the natural connections between impulse and action, such as the one between hunger and eating. We rarely need to suddenly stop everything and make a quick assessment of whether we're hungry or not; at any given point in time, the need for food either makes itself known to us, or else it's not there at all. The same is true for a leg that needs to be moved to prevent cramping, or a bladder that needs to be emptied. What leads to self-correcting behavior is usually instinctive and automatic, a mind-free flow of activity that lends a kind of organic logic to our daily lives.

Sleep is an exception to this scheme. Yes, there is something intuitive and natural about it. We grow tired, so our bodies and minds need to rest. But sleep itself remains a real mystery: we intuit that it's more than just "rest." It seems to be a different realm of being. The craving for sleep can carry the same urgency as feelings of hunger, but lacks a similar straightforward path to resolution. As a consequence, we are quick to be mystified and to relinquish our control to the experts, figuring that they must know more than we do.

Welcome to a modern sleep disorder clinic, a temple to our faith in the medical model. Here, nighttime slumber is the goal, at least to the degree that it can be measured physiologically. An interesting phenomenon that invariably occurs for patients is the "first night effect"; that is, the assessment of any given patient's sleep is almost always different on the first night than on subsequent nights. The first night effect differs from patient to patient: for some, the new environment makes sleep much more difficult. For others, it easily brings slumber because they have escaped their own bedroom, a place associated with nightly struggle. This is the first hint that the problem really lies with the conceptual framework the patients bring with them to the sleep clinic, and not with some physiological problem. Sleep researchers are aware of this phenomenon, but because it doesn't fit their sleep-as-physiology paradigm, this valuable clue is ignored.

The environment in a sleep clinic only serves to reinforce the dominant cultural and scientific explanations of sleep. Patients may feel pressured to achieve sleep (the "duty to sleep," in spades), or worry about what the physiological assessments might portend. The already problematic struggle over maintaining consciousness versus succumbing to sleep may be amplified. And from the patient's perspective — the only one that should matter — such surroundings are anything but conducive to slumber. In someone who is wired to numerous monitors, with a camera recording every movement, how could awareness comfortably fade away? The result is, of course, the diagnosis of whatever variant of insomnia the ensuing physiological measurements indicate. The Thinker wins again. The sleep clinic, despite its altruistic intentions, incarnates the distinctly parental mandate that we need to go to sleep when it's bedtime.

Sleep troubles rank as one of the top reasons for doctor visits. Many patients do everything right according to the experts' advice and still struggle to sleep at night. Strangely enough, there are also many people who do everything *wrong* according to the experts, but who nonetheless sleep soundly every night. More than likely, the explanation lies in the outlook they take to bed with them rather than in the professional advice they've absorbed.

Whether to maintain waking consciousness or not is a private matter, one's own decision, regardless of the mandates of medical science. Because our own sleep has no bearing on anyone else, there is no reason for any person, no matter how much authority they have, to expect us to be either awake or asleep. A famous Zen quote says, "If you meet the Buddha on the road, kill him." This is not meant literally, of course;

it means that anyone claiming to know more than you should not be trusted. Sleep is your own concern — nobody else's.

Need sleep?

Medical "knowledge" about sleep contributes to the overwhelming pressure that insomniacs experience, from without and within, to "accomplish" sleep — so much so that sleep takes on the urgency of a "need." And when one "needs" sleep, the search for it is on. Effort comes into play, along with a host of different responses. A reactive situation is created that triggers the body to become aroused — and there you are, lying in bed wide awake. This whole process takes place internally, but as far as the body's arousal mechanism is concerned, the situation is like any other crisis. The Thinker has fabricated an emergency from the *idea* of sleep, something that exists only in the mind. Does sleep fall into the same "need" category as activities like food gathering and personal safety? If so, little wonder we lie awake at night trying to secure this element vital to our well being. Or have we just become hopelessly ensnared in our mind's tendency to create stories, and forgotten that the nature of consciousness is such that it will move in the direction of sleep if we just leave it alone?

For students of Zen, the concept of "need" is a tricky one. It is a uniquely human idea. When animals sleep, it's not because of any concept of "need." It's just a part of their nature. Why are we so different? One obvious difference is that we have minds that relentlessly separate our experiences into categories and attach labels like "need" — and when something with that particular label goes missing, we panic. What *we think* reality should be and what it really *is* are two different things. So we go about trying to force things to be the way we think they should, never realizing that it is our divisive intellect that creates the suffering in the first place.

The next time that you feel this kind of internal struggle raging, instead of focusing on what the mind says, focus on your experience of the present moment. If you are awake when you are "not supposed to be," so what? The mind will immediately answer that question with a long list of dire consequences. But you don't have to believe in these warnings and respond as though you are a servant to the Thinker — or, worse yet, panic as though you are facing a life-or-death crisis. Simply be in the moment. Allow all that internal talk of "need" to continue if it must, in the background, while keeping the larger part of your attention on the experience of life unfolding in your body and all around you. Pay attention to the real world. The key lesson here is this: However things are, is however things are. Period.

Medical science has clearly lost its way when it comes to sleep: the Thinker has trumped reality. The Buddha would say that we're blind to our true nature, choosing to stuff reality into a mental framework that reduces our existence to biological processes which "should" function correctly, but often don't. Scientific materialism would prevent us from simply experiencing our own sleep in the present moment.

In Zen, one must give up the security of reasoning and venture forth into the uncharted realm of how things really are. We don't yet know what sleep, as a particular manifestation of consciousness, really is. Its true nature — and all of existence, for that matter — is fluid and ever changing, so it cannot be captured and tamed by science. All that we can do is shake free from the hold the Thinker has on us, and explore the wilderness of changing awareness, hopefully without distractions from the self-appointed "experts."

✳

Observations

✳ Notice how science has convinced you that sleep is a bodily function. Can you describe where in the body sleep happens?

✳ How has your intellect colored the experience of rest with ideas of "need"?

✳ Despite your intellect's protest, observe that "sleep" does not actually exist. Now find the courage to trust that observation.

Chapter 4

In the Flow

It is human nature to attempt to control our lives. Most of
our thoughts, words, and actions are geared toward bringing
about a particular outcome, and, as we have seen, the same
desire motivates science. Zen does not exactly counsel us to
give up control: the Buddha's outrageous claim is that we
never had it in the first place, and that our suffering occurs
precisely because of the efforts we make to manufacture it.
When we realize this, our struggles for control naturally
diminish. The challenge, then, is to see things as they really
are. If our notion of control over sleep is an illusion, then perhaps it is not worth clinging to.

How can we once and for all determine if our hopes
for control are misguided? Again, the answer lies in simple,

focused observation. Does sleep start or stop on command? Can you, at this very moment, go to sleep? When slumber does come, is it because you've requested it — or have you merely made yourself ready for it? Close examination will reveal that control over sleep is more a matter of how we wish things to be rather than how they really are.

Our need for control is often the result of fear. Sleep does entail the loss of consciousness, but is there really any danger in that? We can look closely to see if in fact any hazards exist. Be in the moment, and observe the arrival of slumber closely. Because we can find no real threat, perhaps it is our thoughts that create our fear. Does the Thinker label loss of consciousness a "danger"? Such labeling is, after all, what the mind does best — its job, so to speak. Zen respects the functions of the mind, but without necessarily giving it the final say. Can you actually see and point to any lurking danger as awareness begins to fade? If there is no direct observation of a threat, then the mind is simply mistaken. Don't bother to disagree when the Thinker sounds this warning — simply direct your attention toward the truth of what is happening.

It would be easy for the Thinker to begin its strategizing here, jumping to the conclusion that, if the inability to sleep is really an act of avoidance, insomnia can be "cured" by deprogramming our fearfulness and compulsion to control, then reprogramming ourselves to submit willingly to sleep. Notice how the intellect rushes to capture a solution the minute that a new angle is discovered! This maneuver

may or may not be useful. Self-protection is not a simple personality trait that can be turned on and off like a light switch.

Have you ever tried to tell yourself to *not* feel hungry when you're hungry? This kind of command tends to have the opposite effect, usually making you focus even more on your hunger pangs. If sleep is to ever become a natural experience, it cannot be dealt with in the context of self-control. Trying to will yourself to give up your opposition to sleep is a mental gymnastic, and will inevitably create more internal struggle. If you've ever tried, you know it can't be done.

Meeting sleep

The Buddha said that we can eliminate the need for such mind-games through the process of careful self-awareness. Place your attention in the present moment. Observe how the mind creates an "I" and then an "it" (sleep), and bestows upon the latter an aura of danger, or perhaps of some mysterious power that must somehow be confronted. The Buddha would be quick to point out that this is the usual conceptual battleground: the more power given to the Thinker, the more confusion and suffering one will experience.

If you've been following along this far, you may have already figured out the next step: to experiment with meeting the experience of sleep on its own terms. This is a fresh perspective that lies outside the realms of the Thinker's mental grappling, our scientific theorizing, and our emotional long-ing for solutions, and it could bring us the kind of intuitive knowledge that infants possess. Newborns are free of the adult framework that stipulates that the absence of external aware-ness — what we often call "sleep" — must itself be a separate state to be analyzed and practiced.

For thinking adults, this means throwing in the towel. Conceding the defeat of science and reason is not easy. To think of meeting sleep on its own turf, with no guidelines or theories, is somewhat daunting, but it can be done. It involves starting in the present, on square one, with an open mind and without regard for anything you think you know about sleep.

On "not doing" sleep

When someone asks, "How did you sleep?" what are they inferring? Examine this question closely. It contains an assumption so widely accepted as fact that it's rarely ques-tioned, and is revealed by the key word "did." This word is the past tense of "do," and therein lays our error — we either consciously or subconsciously believe sleep to be something we "do."

On the surface, it could seem true enough. Isn't it obvi-ous that sleep is something a person "does"? We talk about sleep as though it were an activity, and our use of language reflects that: for example, our use of words like "inability" to

describe not being able to "do" sleep. But this whole suppo-
sition is fundamentally false. Sleep is in fact a complete ces-
sation of "doing." Look closely at your experience of sleep,
just as a Zen Buddhist would. Point to the "doing" in sleep.
If you can't, then how do you know it is there?

The initial mistaken assumption goes on to breed even
more misconceptions. If sleep is seen as an activity, then we
optimistically assume that it can be improved with some type
of skill-building exercises, which, as we have seen, rarely work.
There is no way to change these social misconstructions, and
trying to force the realization that sleep is not "doing" into a
cognitive format only creates a vacuum. But it *is* possible for
us to directly experience the truth that sleep is essentially an
inner invitation to "*stop* doing."

In the Zen tradition, there is a saying that "The right
view is simply that view which is not any one particular view."
This means an outlook not colored by beliefs, concepts, opinions, or ideals; it is a vision free from the mind's obstructions.
To observe sleep without using the mind is to see clearly that
there is no "doing" there. That is the "right view" the Buddha
spoke of.

Sensing the reality that there is no "doing" in sleep is
gradual. "Doing sleep" is an idea in the realm of the mind,
while "not doing" describes the effortlessness of drifting
towards sleep. Our modern lives have become so attuned to
reacting to demands and achieving goals that there is no place
for a request to simply stop all activity. Our memories and

future speculations are made up of action and reaction, demand and fulfillment, deadline and detour. How often do we receive a message to simply *stop* everything we're doing and just *be?*

The next time someone asks, "How did you sleep?" pause for a moment and translate this assumption-based question to a more accurate reality-based one: "How did sleep *happen to you?*" From that perspective you can offer a real response, even if the questioner might remain stuck in the fundamental misunderstanding that sleep is something that one "does."

Of course, others around you may not see that sleep involves no activity. How could they? In the Information Age, when so much of our activity consists of mind-work, the very notion of "doing" usually implies cognitive effort, especially regarding things we associate with the mind, like sleep. This observation carries us one step beyond our earlier conclusions about the concept of sleep. We saw how the modern world increases the amount of time we spend thinking, thus turning the experience of sleep into a concept. Now that we've discovered the "doing" aspect of our trap, we notice how the concept of "doing sleep" compels us even further inward, away from reality — because "inward" is where much of our modern doing takes place. If most of our "doing" is not taking place "out there" in the world of direct experience, but instead "in here" — in the mind — we are dangerously close to irretrievably losing sight of reality altogether.

Moreover, we have lost the habit of simply *looking* outwardly *or* inwardly. Given the relatively small number of demands on our attention from the physical world compared with the enormous increase in the demand to think and "figure it out," this is hardly surprising. As a result of no longer having the time to *look,* our misperceptions feed on one another without detection. Our cognitive material tends to form snarled webs of relationships that block the natural flow of consciousness. So it's worth repeating the advice that Buddha gave us: Open your eyes. Pay attention.

Dreams

Instead of falling into the same "doing" trap with dreams — as in, "What did you dream last night?" — let's take a step back and look only at what can actually be observed in the world of dreams. On a physiological level, electrical impulses flit through the brain, combining and recombining at varying magnitudes and intervals. The resulting dreams create an alternate realm that often parallels the external world. Certain conflicts based in our waking world may get worked out here in ways that may seem bizarre to the conscious mind. In fact, none of the rules of the external world apply: dreamscape is a place where anything can happen.

The vivid realism of many dreams is evidence that, from an experiential point of view, the external world and the dream world are interchangeable: both are subjectively experienced as real-time, authentic events. We see, hear, act, and feel in a dream. People refer to "good" or "bad" dreams. We all like a good dream, and nobody likes a bad dream. A good dream can leave us in a good mood, and a bad dream can do the opposite. This confirms — if we didn't already know — that we are living, feeling beings who are affected by all of the events in our experiential reality.

Assuming that you're awake right now, you might protest that dreams don't carry the same validity as events in your "real" waking life. Yet in the midst of intense dreaming, there is normally no awareness that the experience is a dream. And most of us have experienced that disconcerting stage of awakening where we're not sure exactly where we are, or if what we just experienced while asleep actually happened.

If any experience — in dreams or elsewhere — is simply too peculiar to be "real," we're tempted to conclude that it didn't happen. If it was plausible but unlikely, we'll probably cautiously investigate. Occasionally we may even register a memory from a dream as something that's actually happened to us, and become confused when external facts don't reflect what we believe took place. The final determination of a particular event's "realness" is made not in the moment of the experience itself, but in the domain of probabilities: our minds swiftly and instinctively calculate the chances of a thing actually having occurred the way it seemed to. So apparently we need the Thinker after all, to decide what side of the fence an experience falls on.

And this is a most worthwhile function of the intellect — as long as it doesn't destroy the freshness of our experience once the calculations begin. To label an event "a dream" fundamentally alters the experience, erasing its potential significance in the service of our adult minds' need for the safety of a well-categorized world — a world we can immediately understand, so that we can quickly move on to the next challenge, the next obligation. Prior to learning this mental routine, we viewed the world through the eyes of a child; each experience was as valid and worthwhile as any other. And dreams were no exception.

Now, as grown-ups, we often sweep the memory of a dream under the rug, and sometimes we can't even remember our dreams. But on some level we know that dreams have happened, that our mind simply turned inward and created its own world. When our consciousness returns to the external world, only fragments remain of what we experienced while submerged in that mysterious other world. Many of us experience our waking life the same way: the individual moments and events that made up our day are, by evening, either completely lost to us, or else have become a blur of half-remembered bits of light and sound and meaning, to perhaps re-emerge later on, in our dream-world.

And dreaming is not exclusively limited to the times we're asleep. Many people have daydreams, some of which are so potent that they drown out the external world. We don't normally completely withdraw our attention from the outer world during the day, but when we do, we'll call it a nap if it is short and deep enough. If we're sitting upright, with our eyes open and our mind turned inward, then we say we're daydreaming.

Daydreaming is not identical to night-dreaming. Someone who is daydreaming can quickly refocus their attention outwardly, either of their own volition or because of some external trigger — unlike the more lengthy process of waking up from a deep slumber. Still, the differences between sleep and waking are less absolute than we would believe. We're usually — but not always — unaware of the outside world when asleep, and usually — but not always — aware of the external when awake.

Individuals who are quietly daydreaming seldom disturb those around them. But what if a person is actively engaged in their dream-world encounter, but is wide awake and interacting with their physical environment, perhaps mixing elements of both worlds together? Those who can't distinguish between the external and internal worlds are labeled "psychotic," because they seem to be reacting to things that don't exist. It's interesting to note that those things they're reacting to differ little from ordinary dreams, both daydreams and night-dreams, in terms of their content. What they may be lacking is that mechanism that summons the Thinker, who can then automatically make those crucial calculations that distinguish between the practical "real" world and mind-stuff.

Even in psychotic states there is still some awareness of the external world, since the individual is usually able to move about in their environment and make a few appropriate connections with people and situations, even while hallucinations are ongoing. The fact that hallucinations are a frequent consequence of sleep deprivation suggests there is some connection between the experiences of night dreaming, day dreaming, and hallucinating. And now the Thinker *really* demands an explanation! What could the missing links be? As we've discovered, most of the mysteries of consciousness lie outside the Thinker's domain, so the solution to this riddle must come from our direct experience. Can we sense the connections?

First of all, we've seen that the three types of dreaming can feel alike subjectively. In fact, close examination will reveal that events in those realms actually can feel just the same as events taking place during periods of ordinary waking consciousness. Because of this, there are times when we have doubts about which category a particular memory or perception belongs to, asking ourselves, "Was it only a dream?" or, "Did I really just see what I thought I saw?" Only deep, completely dreamless slumber feels qualitatively different — that being a sort of nothingness. Aside from this, the fact is that all of our other experiencing ebbs and flows with a surprising quality of underlying sameness. The Thinker may be frightened by this observation; it erases all the neat divisions we so carefully construct to divide up the many ways that our consciousness manifests itself.

Whatever differences there may be come not from the experiences themselves, but from how we view them. Or more precisely, how the Thinker (and the other Thinkers around us) views them. The mind's system of identification tells us not what is actually happening inside — where it all feels pretty much the same — but more about where our body and awareness are located when a given event in our consciousness takes place. So if we are tucked into bed, it's late at night, and we suddenly wake up from some experience, the Thinker immediately jumps in to reassure us that "it was just a dream." And hallucinations are classed as "symptoms of disease" if they don't occur in the context of sleep. Perhaps psychosis is only dreaming that doesn't confine itself to appropriate times. And maybe the so-called "healthy" individuals are those who dream only when society says they should, mostly at night and with no concurrent awareness of the external — and occasionally during the day when awake, but without any noticeable and "inappropriate" interactions with our dream-stuff.

After this survey of dreaming, the Thinker will immediately want to inquire about the "real significance" of dreams. But we have already seen that significance is a value created by the mind because of our intellect's craving for a meaning, an explanation, something rational to be guided by. If we have the courage to question this yearning, we will find that it's not really our whole *being* that yearns, but just the intellect, a small part of ourselves. Verify this for yourself by *seeing* that the issue arises from the Thinker's demands for answers, rather than a real curiosity about dreaming itself.

We may have an occasional nightmare, but for the most part dreaming provides enjoyment — satisfactions very comparable to those we get from day-to-day living. A particularly good or interesting dream is preserved for later enjoyment just like any other pleasant memory. If the Thinker is unsatisfied with its inability to find some stable ground here, so what? Dreaming, after all, need not be subjected to intellectual analysis any more than what occurs during the daytime. Do we always try to investigate and classify our waking experiences? Of course we don't. The depth and fulfillment of our waking life can never be captured by intellectual explanations precisely because it's our *reality*, not something conceptual. The latter misses the point of the former: both our dreaming and waking lives demand to be *experienced*, not packaged by the intellect. Is the time we spend dreaming so very different qualitatively than our hours spent awake?

The Thinker says absolutely! Dividing and labeling is its stock-in-trade. We'll take a closer look at this in the next chapter. For now, simply experiment with this other way of seeing. See if you can observe not separate, carefully labeled

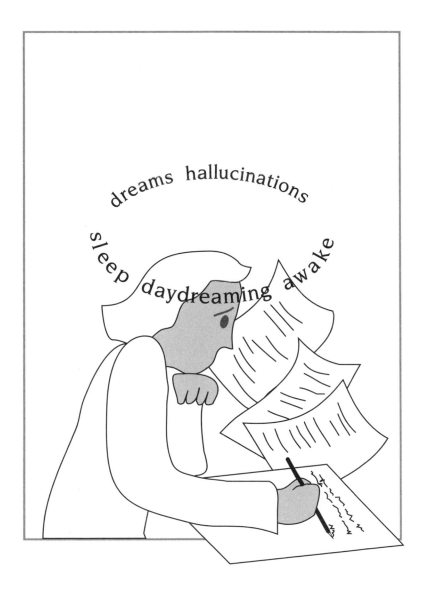

entity-events, but one continuously changing stream of consciousness. Our new, nonacademic understanding of the nature of sleep unfolds slowly. Our path is not a straight one, but rather one that continuously circles back to bring forward insights discovered earlier in the process. This reflects the start-and-go quality of enlightenment, which can occur with either slight changes in perspective or sudden exclamations of, "Eureka, I see!"

There will be times when, in using words to communicate, we must employ the language of the mind. Now that we've explored some of the big picture, the word "sleep" can begin to point to a place on the changing spectrum of consciousness. It may still be a word and a concept, but now it contains some new ideas that reflect reality more accurately. Because the word itself carries much of the old cognitive baggage, as we continue our exploration and the word "sleep" occurs, try alternating between the two kinds of understandings, the conceptual and the experiential. This will get easier as we continue to unfold the enlightened perspective on sleep.

As awareness shifts

When our awareness begins its cyclic shift away from the outer world, the Thinker labels that experience "drowsy." This fatigue of the mind causes less strife for our intellect than sleep does, probably because there still remains at least some focus on the outer environment. But, we ask, why does awareness change its direction in the first place? That is the Thinker, once again asking questions. All that we can observe, and thus all that matters — because reality *is* all that matters — is that this seems to be the fundamental nature of consciousness. It comes and goes, ebbs and flows.

Redefining the experience we call "getting drowsy" as "consciousness inevitably changing its direction, away from the external world" throws the Thinker for a loop. Indeed, even calling awareness "a stream that ebbs and flows" presents a problem. As we know, the mind wants everything to be static, fixed at a particular point in time at a particular place, and preferably amenable to being measured and categorized.

Because of their unceasing flux, most aspects of consciousness elude our every attempt to explain them. Obviously, awareness exists — "it" is looking at this page at this very moment. This fact will register with the Thinker momentarily, but not for long. When your awareness shifts, it is best described as a change in direction — not that this captures the process, for we know that reality cannot be captured with words. But the ongoing change in direction throughout the day, which inevitably bring us to the moment in time that we call "getting drowsy," is not in itself a problem — unless the Thinker makes it one.

How will it happen to me?

Deep within yourself, you've discovered that sleepiness and sleep are both events that happen whether you want them to or not. Again, observe the experience of drowsiness, this time on two levels. First, watch how your awareness of the surroundings diminishes. This is our experience of a flow that, as we have said, is best left to its own devices. As we have discovered, this shift in awareness requires no effort and poses no difficulty. Here is reality, the natural flow that Zen is after.

Then go ahead and translate this same process into mind-speak: you notice that drowsiness comes to you, rather than being something that you actively solicit. Try to find it, and it will hide. Try to avoid it, and it will eventually appear of its own accord. This is how the mind views the events in our lives, as separate entities interacting with one another, and often at odds. This is a reflection of our troubled relationship with whatever we consider to be both highly desirable and maddeningly elusive.

Our tendency to go with the mind-based version of sleep unfortunately obscures our deeper understanding of the former approach — which is not a "version" at all. Reality lies in the *experience,* beyond the reach of words. Slowly but surely, we can change the meaning of the words we use so they more accurately reflect reality, even if they are a rather poor substitute.

With these insights, you can begin to perceive sleep's true nature — or, more accurately, the true nature of consciousness in the particular form we label "sleep." A shift in the flow of consciousness is not a separate and discrete "thing," despite what our minds might tell us. We may not see the whole picture yet, so this perspective could still seem perplexing. Keep at it, and reality will slowly reveal herself.

Try approaching bedtime tonight with the question, "How will sleep happen to me tonight?" Or for those who can already *see,* "How will my consciousness shift its direction tonight?" Perhaps drowsiness and then sleep will happen to you in a light, fleeting way, taking you through continual shifts and changes in your experience. Perhaps sleep will not visit you at all. Or maybe it will arrive with such speed that within a few minutes you are deep in slumber without being aware of the transition. To participate in sleep in this new way, all that you need to remember is this: However it happens is all right. How sleep arrives is, as we have observed, beyond your control. Tomorrow will arrive no matter what sleep chooses to do tonight. In the morning, plan to ask yourself, "How did sleep happen to me last night?" Understand that sleep *happens,* coming to visit you with or without an invitation. There is nothing for you to "do." You don't even need to put out the welcome mat unless you want to.

A famous disciple of the Buddha said it best: To carry yourself forward and experience myriad things is delusion; That myriad things come forth and experience themselves is awakening. In other words, actively trying to capture an experience — or even looking for an explanation — only disrupts the natural flow of consciousness from this moment to the next moment. There is nothing to "do" or "know" about sleep.

If, on the other hand, you view sleep in the usual way, as something separate from yourself that you're individually responsible for, as something that you "do," then you won't be able to accommodate yourself to flowing in the underlying realm of an ever-changing consciousness. Your mind's habitual patterns will ensure that the focus remains on *you, your* reactions, *your* thoughts — particularly your concepts of sleep — instead of where it should be, on the present moment . . . which may or may not unfold the way you would like.

This new approach — to not take any particular approach — brings us into what is, at its heart, a relatively impersonal realm where there is no sense of a "you" acquiring sleep. But, once again, upon close inspection we find that this is not a problem. The Thinker will insist that it is, because the old mental framework stipulates there must be a "you" as hunter and "sleep" as the prey. But now that we have sensed the true nature of consciousness — that it ebbs and flows on its own — we may know better.

Let's take a breather, as we've covered quite a bit of ground in the last several chapters. By now you have a better sense of what a Zen approach to sleep is all about. If you look closely, you'll see that you have come further *toward where you already are.* To understand the nature of consciousness *is* enlightenment. The rest of the journey you'll be taking in this book isn't particularly arduous; it does, however, take persistence in order to realize the whole picture. In the next chapter, we'll be going where the Zen masters go, so take a deep breath and keep reading.

✳

Observations

✳ Notice how you might assume responsibility for sleep. Then see if, in some way, you frame sleep as an activity or skill. Try instead to experience that sleep just occurs on its own.

✳ Remember a favorite dream and how real it seemed at the time. Now recall an event that happened during your waking hours. Can you sense how both memories are similar?

✳ When you begin to explore the ebb and flow of your awareness, how do you feel? Observe how your mind tries to take over, labeling the changes as somehow separate and perhaps something that you must control.

✳ Pay attention to your present level of alertness. At this moment does it seem to be increasing, decreasing, or staying about the same? Try to formulate a response that doesn't contain any language that is judgmental ("that is bad"), comparing ("this is better than I felt before"), or that refers to *you*: for example, rather than "I'm tired," say "There is sleepiness now."

Chapter 5

Beyond the Self Who Sleeps

To take oneself out of the picture and allow the flow of consciousness to unfold — without the motive to acquire sleep — might seem rather puzzling to you. The very purpose of reading this book is, after all, to obtain a good night's rest. How could we undertake this journey in order to heal our problems with sleep, only to end with the conclusion that we never needed to do so the first place?

Because now we *see* our situation. Finally we understand the heart of the problem that the Buddha pointed out: it's not the various shifts in awareness that we call waking and sleep that plague us, but our own intellect, that one small part of our being that we've permitted to overshadow our direct participation in reality. The path that leads us out of this situation takes time and practice. For many, Buddhist meditation offers a way to this freedom from the mind. Our objective, as we've said before, is not to eliminate or control the intellect, but rather to simply *observe* how it works.

Dualizing

Mind-activity is like a one-way street — and it always leads us to opposites. Try this thought-experiment. Think about temperature, and you'll end up thinking in terms of either hot or cold. Think about size, and you wind up with big or small. Think about consciousness, and you end up dividing it into either "awake" or "asleep."

A close examination of these concepts reveals that, in keeping with the mind's polarizing tendency, they will appear on the cognitive stage *only* in pairs. If you take away the idea of hot, there can be no idea of cold. Take away big, and small disappears. And in the context of our particular discussion, we invariably define sleep by what it is not, namely "awake." By definition, a concept will always have an opposite, and our minds will always bounce between the two, unaware of the fluid nature of reality that lies outside. This small bit of understanding can take us a long way towards freedom from the Thinker's habits.

There are, of course, different gradations between the two opposite poles of any given spectrum, but even these gray areas still exist entirely in the mind and so are susceptible to becoming polarized. Think for a moment about the "right size" of some article of clothing. That "rightness" of size is determined precisely by what it is *not*, namely too big or too small. We can permit the Thinker to do its assigned jobs — like making these kinds of comparisons — but we don't have to give up the deeper and more significant reality of the moment. *Feel* that sensation you call temperature, *wear* that article of clothing, and *permit* consciousness to go where it goes. These kinds of organic, noncognitive connections to the larger world transcend anything the experts can offer. Their vision is that of the Thinker — everything reduced to parts that can be fiddled with in an attempt to improve performance.

The illusion of self

Because our deeper understandings don't consist of parts, there's nothing to fiddle with. Ultimate enlightenment in Zen — what every serious student attempts to realize — is the liberation from the illusion of self. This is an especially perplexing aim for Westerners because, as we have discovered, so much of modern activity involves a notion of "self" as either the instigator of action or the recipient of it. On various levels, especially socially, that mind-thing which we call "identity" carries tremendous weight. And on a day-to-day basis there is obviously *someone* who goes to work, cleans the bathroom, and tries to fall asleep at night. Right?

In the mind-realm, that's true. If we take a step back in order to look at the larger picture, without assigning meanings to any one element, we can observe our selves — individual manifestations of the universal — going about in what we imagine to be our own private worlds, unaware of every moment giving birth to the next, and that every so-called "part" has boundaries only because our awareness is so limited. The "all" — one continuous stream — can still be sensed, even though it cannot be registered intellectually.

Given the dualizing nature of the thinking mind, we inevitably see the world in terms of *in here* versus *out there.* In this way, we are viewing reality through a warped lens that causes us to feel a profound separateness from the world. It's little surprise that we struggle with existential questions because of this illusion, often turning to religion for help. The fact that everything is interdependently connected, woven from the same fabric — *no* "in here" or "out there"— can be directly perceived only by participating in the moment-to-moment flow of life. Our spiritual nature ensures that we *can sense* our connection to the whole, even if words fail miserably to describe it. There is — in reality — no separate "self" to be either awake or asleep.

We tend to assume that all that exists is a separate, individual human body, which the mind claims is "mine." But can you identify the *me* in "mine"? Try simply pointing to yourself. Carefully observe that you have pointed to one element of the universe, a body. Now point to *whose* body it is. Do you see?

Look at a photograph of yourself at a very young age. Is that *you?* Hold that picture up in front of a mirror to compare it with your reflection. Although the mind will insist that it's you, observe the substantial differences. If the "you" in the picture is not the same "you" in the mirror, then *where* is that one continuous, separate "self" that you insist upon? Bodies, like the universe itself, are in a constant state of change. The Thinker takes the easy way out, and calls it "growing old."

Look at your name: it's a series of words, a concept that has been reinforced by a lifetime of social interactions. Say your name out loud. What you've just voiced is an idea that exists in the mind. Point to your name — and don't cheat by pointing to your body. Components of the universe can be pointed to, because they exist; concepts can't be pointed to because they don't exist, *except in the mind.*

New students of Zen are sometimes terrified at being unable to directly locate a "self" — until they realize what a blessing that is. Existential questions about birth, death, and meaning all disappear when the truth is discerned from amidst all the mental noise. One glimpse, and all the heavy questions about "my purpose" seem to vanish. As reality becomes more our day-to-day experience, remnants of the initial fears fade away, often replaced by giggling over this ultimate trick of the intellect. "I" was never born to begin with!

Yes, a body was born, or more accurately, that current which is the "all" sent forth another new stream, the separate identity of which is created by the mind. It might seem strange to look upon our human bodies simply as parts of the larger universe, because we've added so many meanings along the way in order to create a self. And this is a necessary, valuable part of being social creatures. Our individual selves do exist, socially — just not within the larger reality that Zen shows us. Zen masters sleep — or don't sleep — peacefully because they're not saddled with concepts like "self" or "sleep."

The wisdom of children

In this way, Zen masters are like young children who have not yet developed a sense of self. Without this added burden, the flow of awareness from moment to moment proceeds unimpeded. At an early age, experiences are not seen as "separate" from the one who experiences them, precisely because there is no "self" to do the experiencing. That artificial division between the "self" and "everything else" is created later on in our cognitive development. Our adult minds will have trouble with this until we momentarily become selfless — breaking through the illusion of self — and experience what children, who have not yet given the Thinker so much control, already know.

It can be illuminating at this point to observe how the intellect might demand a full accounting of what exactly it is that children "already know," expecting it to be in a form that makes sense intellectually. Yet we have discovered that children's wisdom is inherently nonintellectual. It turns out that humans don't need *any* version of sleep, or of the "self," for that matter, in order to get by.

The delightful flow of unobstructed consciousness manifests itself most easily in children. And why wouldn't it? New life, no matter the species, embodies energy and excitement. The satisfaction of being one with the world — not the social concept of the world that we adults have, but the literal reality that children experience — makes the world an easy and even awesome place to live. An infinite number of influences gather together at one point in time and cause the young child to squeal with the sheer joy of it all. Later, this bundle of energy will change direction and quiet down. Constant change, after all, characterizes everything. Therein lies the flow.

For newborns, who sail right along in the flow, not the slightest bit of structure exists in consciousness. Once their needs are met, it takes only seconds for an infant to go right back to sleep. Obviously, there are no skills or understandings involved in this process. If that were the case, older people would find sleep more easily than the very young.

For us grown-ups, it takes considerable spiritual gumption to reconnect to that earlier era of enlightenment and in effect say to our over-indulged intellect, "Yes, keep on insisting there is a 'me' that 'does' sleep or waking" — and then proceed to connect with the flow of the moment, knowing that our awareness will change direction on its own.

Letting go

Because the flow of awareness is in constant flux — the antithesis of the static world of ideas — it threatens the Thinker. This is a frequent challenge for those new at meditation. Quietly observing your awareness can be like watching a four-year-old: neither patient nor focused, awareness will always divert itself to something else, and from there to something else again. At some point, it will turn its focus away from the outer world altogether, which is another aspect of its elusive nature — and probably is the reason you're reading this book. While a Buddhist merely observes all the different aspects of this flow, the intellect wants none of it.

Sleep is the last straw for the Thinker, completely eluding all attempts to define and control it. Now that we're aware of the underlying reality of what we're observing, the frustrations of the Thinker need not take on so much importance. Its ramblings need not interrupt the flow.

They might at first, of course. Relegating a part of ourselves that has always been in the driver's seat to the back seat requires us to adjust. For some time to come, the tendency will be for the Thinker to call the shots, so expect that thoughts about the awake-to-asleep spectrum will make an

appearance in the evening and possibly in the morning, along with stern warnings about the "need" to move from one end to the other. Eventually, all this will become mere background noise. Over time, it can easily be let go altogether.

For we have started to make peace with *the way things are.* By being alert to what is actually happening with regard to sleep, and exploring the very nature of how we understand ourselves, our situation has become much clearer. We have come full circle, ready to let go of the misguided assumption that we are on a mission to capture sleep.

As it turns out, securing sleep is a conceptual red herring. The Buddha warned us long ago that our minds would create this kind of unnecessary suffering. Only by accurately perceiving our condition in the moment is enlightenment possible. Then we can make those first steps, however awkwardly, to assign the Thinker a more appropriate support role. This realignment of the chain of command becomes easier the more aware we become of the mind's strengths and limitations. Perhaps for making comparisons in the physical world, our mind's ability to capture a moment and then scrutinize and evaluate it is invaluable. For anything else — and there is considerably more — we need our deepest awareness to tap into the more substantial truths.

As spiritual beings, we *know* that true wisdom is found not in the intellectual realms, but in experiencing the present moment. And what a wonderful moment we find ourselves in. We are able to reclaim what is naturally ours: the serenity of a consciousness ebbing and flowing in whatever direction it happens to be moving at the time. The answer was here all along, and now, as the Buddha would say, we can see.

✳

Observations

✳ When you begin to see your "self" as an illusion, what feelings come up?

✳ Remember your own child-wisdom, before there was a "you," before there was "sleep." Now find that nonintellectual memory arising from the language of sensations. Verify there *is* a memory from before the "self," even if words cannot describe it.

✳ Confirm that there is no inherent problem with changes in awareness. How loudly, if at all, does your intellect protest that observation?

Conclusion

Enlightenment rarely happens on its own. It requires our consistent attention to the ways that the mind supersedes our deeper sense of being. Not that we want to reject the mind which, as we have discovered, has its own valuable roles, but we want to discern where a deeper understanding might be found. Given our tendency to accept mind-based concepts as our gospel truth, observing our world with "bare attention" — without any accompanying interpretations — may feel awkward. Rarely do we reflect on the simple but profound fact that "how things are is how things are," and that this elusive reality is our true starting point.

Remember that the "right view" of Zen is perspective-free. It inquires into everything, with no preconceptions or understandings of any kind. Because this approach of *not taking any particular approach* can initially seem so paradoxical, we started our journey with some introductory discussion of Zen Buddhism. And at first we were unable to locate a Zen explanation of sleep. Only gradually did we realize there was a deeper truth awaiting our discovery, one that didn't involve theories or interpretations.

We reached this insight by contrasting our mental baggage — such as our nagging sense of a "duty" to sleep — with a quiet observation of reality. Not only were there no obligations to be found, but all of our assumed connections between sleep and success in daily life turned out to be spurious. The Thinker was busy interpreting the sequential order of events in ways that created a tremendous sense of pressure, using mere ideas that couldn't even be verified in the real world. This plunge into the deep end of Zen may have felt rather unsettling at the time, but it did show us the value and power of our own direct observations.

Having gotten our toes wet, we went on to examine how cultural influences have shaped our beliefs about sleep. Value judgments grow like weeds when it comes to this subject, and it was relatively easy to confirm how useless they are. Sleep, it turns out, comes on its own timetable and in its own way. What few choices we have about sleep seem to have more to do with how we accommodate ourselves to the arrival of sleep than with strategies that would directly affect sleep itself.

Remembering how we accepted sleep when we were children, in an earlier era of trust, opened a valuable door. But we still needed to reflect on our present-time, adult relationship with sleep and the ways that modern life has made it so difficult. Perhaps for the first time, we discovered the overwhelming dominance of thinking and conceptualizing in our daily lives, and how they can distort the actual experience of sleep, transforming it from a simple experience into one concept among many others in our repertoire. Slowly we began to see our predicament.

Turning next towards our era's dominant roadmap to sleep, science, we observed how the model of sleep as a bodily function fuels an institution called sleep medicine. This flies in the face of our actual experience of sleep, which suggests that something more than mere biology is at play. Close inspection revealed how nothing of sleep actually exists to be measured, contrary to the conceptual models employed by the sleep experts. We took a close look at their way of thinking, especially the notion of "need," and watched how the mind so often uses that concept as a springboard to create all manner of interruptions in the flow of awareness.

Up to this point, we'd had only a few glimpses of the nature of the ebb and flow of consciousness. Having already begun to sense it, we knew in a new, nonacademic way that what we labeled "sleep" was simply another form of continuously changing consciousness. The Thinker was still protesting, of course, but not so loudly. Soon we realized the need to meet sleep on its own terms, so we stepped up to the plate.

Finally, the "right view" of Zen started to make sense. It was not so much a matter of examining a particular event or thing as much as discovering the *nature* of what it is we were looking for and the most useful way to look. Having begun our journey with no particular approach, discarding our pre-conceptions along the way, it became possible to discover that what we were seeking moves along under its own power, requiring absolutely no participation by us. We now had a much clearer sense of the flow as something completely outside of our control, and manifested most comfortably when we stop "doing" sleep — or anything else.

Watching the various ways that consciousness manifests itself led us to further insights. Artificial divisions between dreaming and normal day-to-day experiences break down when we sense how similar are all the events in our lives. And as we began to see the larger picture — that consciousness may be constantly changing, but it is all of the same fabric — the source of our suffering is much easier to identify. Clearly, it is the Thinker who dislikes the way things are — unlike our inner spiritual being, which finds the unfolding of the universe so immensely satisfying.

Lastly, we touched on the most valuable potential of Zen, that of becoming selfless. With neither a "self" as hunter nor a "sleep" as prey, our awareness flows in an effortless fashion, moving in a manner completely in sync with the larger stream. This is our rightful place beside all other living creatures, and waits only to be rediscovered.

When observing that the source of our problem lies with the adult cognitive boundaries that separate and solidify the different manifestations of consciousness, we are tempted to think that this is a new system that we should either believe or disbelieve. The Thinker will even want to create new concepts based on these observations, a sort of "Zen version" of sleep. But, as we have seen, a worldview that is captured by a set of beliefs or concepts can never match reality itself, simply because reality is not frozen. Our reasoning — and its offspring, science — insists that essential truths can be captured within a particular conceptual framework, ignoring our deeper intuitions, which inform us about the fluid and flexible nature of existence. The Buddha understood this, and saw how enlightenment flows only from direct, mind-free, moment-to-moment experience.

Therefore, we should be cautious about assuming that *Zen Sleep* represents reality. This rather formless little tome, the pages of which offer neither academic explanations of sleep nor methodologies to "acquire" sleep, will act at best like a compass pointing us in the right direction to look. No book can capture reality, because *any* explanation will, by the very fact that it is a construction of the mind, lack the validity of the real thing. Instead, *Zen Sleep* offers us a life raft across the rough waters of our intellect. Once on the other side, it is best to leave the raft behind. Otherwise we might confuse the raft, simply a means to an end, with what we actually came to see — the reality of our experience.

And at some point even our focus on the experience we call sleep will no longer be useful. Given its freedom, consciousness flows along through its many forms rather freely, needing no particular attention, and certainly not our constant monitoring. For once our situation is seen, nothing remains to be done, except perhaps for just letting it all go.

For in the end, this is a journey to enjoy, rediscovering what we already instinctively know. It's just a matter of waking up to our situation, as the Buddha would say, to see the way things really are, the surprisingly comfortable and harmonious movement of consciousness that always proceeds in the right direction at the right time, with no assistance required. This must be why the Buddha laughed so frequently. It's all so very easy, despite the minor distractions Thinker might come up with. Now we know. Now we are enlightened.

✳

Give the gift of sleep enlightenment

* Order additional copies of *Zen Sleep* for family and friends.

* Call 1-800-247-6553 or purchase online at www.ZenSleep.info